THE CHALLENGE OF THE AMERICAN DREAM:

The Chinese in the United States

MINORITIES IN AMERICAN LIFE SERIES

General Editor: Alexander DeConde
University of California, Santa Barbara

THE IRISH IN THE UNITED STATES, John B. Duff, Seton Hall University

THE CHALLENGE OF THE AMERICAN DREAM: THE CHINESE IN THE UNITED STATES, Francis L. K. Hsu, Northwestern University

FORTHCOMING

THE SOCIETY AND CULTURE OF THE MEXICAN AMERICANS, Jesus Chavarria, University of California, Santa Barbara

THE AMERICAN POLES, Louis L. Gerson, University of Connecticut

BLACK URBAN AMERICA SINCE RECONSTRUCTION, Hollis R. Lynch, Columbia University

THE JAPANESE AMERICAN, Setsuko M. Nishi, Brooklyn College

JEWISH CULTURE IN THE UNITED STATES IN THE 20TH CENTURY, Milton Plesur, State University of New York at Buffalo

ITALIAN CULTURE AND HISTORY IN THE UNITED STATES, Andrew F. Rolle, Occidental College

THE NEGRO CULTURE IN THE SOUTH SINCE THE CIVIL WAR, Arnold H. Taylor, University of Connecticut

THE CHALLENGE OF THE AMERICAN DREAM:

The Chinese in the United States

FRANCIS L. K. HSU

NORTHWESTERN UNIVERSITY

WADSWORTH PUBLISHING COMPANY, INC., BELMONT, CALIFORNIA

L. C. Cat. Card No.:
71–170311
ISBN–0–534–00043–6

Printed in the United States of
America

1 2 3 4 5 6 7 8 9 10—
75 74 73 72 71

SERIES PREFACE

The *Minorities in American Life* series is designed to illuminate hitherto-neglected areas of America's cultural diversity. Each author treats problems, areas, groups, or issues that cannot ordinarily be examined in depth in the usual surveys of American history and related subjects. Although all the volumes are connected to each other through the unifying theme of minority cultures, the series is flexible and open to a number of uses. For example, two or more volumes can be used as units in a comparative study. Each will bring out the distinctive features of an ethnic group, but together the books may show the common as well as the unique features and experiences of each minority studied.

In varying degrees every book includes narrative, analysis, and interpretation. Each is written simply, clearly, and intelligently by an authority on its subject, and all reflect the most recent scholarship. Some restate, with fresh insights, what scholars may already know; others present new syntheses, little-known data, or original ideas related to old concepts; and all are intended to stimulate thought, not merely to pass on information. By opening minority studies to young people, the series also meets a social and educational need. By providing short, sound, and readable books on their life and culture, and by accepting them on their own terms, the series accords minorities the justice and appreciation for their heritage that they have seldom received. By dealing with live issues in a historical context, it also makes the role of minority culture in American life meaningful to young people and opens new doors to an understanding of the American past and present.

Alexander DeConde

PREFACE

This is not a book on the history of the Chinese in the United States, where they are located, or how poorly or well they have done. Consequently statistical figures and detailed factual descriptions have been kept to a minimum. Instead, I have attempted to see the situation of the Chinese in the United States in terms of contact and conflict between two vastly different ways of life: how Chinese and White Americans conduct themselves under the circumstances; the effect of such contact and conflict on the behavior patterns of the individual; and what future course Chinese–Americans and White Americans should pursue in mutual accommodation for a brighter and happier America of tomorrow.

For better understanding I have also used researches on other minority groups (for example, Jewish–Americans), rather than confine the discussion to the Chinese case alone. My hope is that the results will illuminate the situation of all minority groups in America, not just that of the Chinese.

I first visited Hawaii and did research among Hawaiian–Chinese in 1949–1950. My most recent visit to the Islands was in 1969–1970. During the two decades between these visits, I lived mostly in the Midwest, but traveled quite extensively in different parts of the United States and Canada and developed a certain degree of acquaintance with the Chinese in many cities including New York, San Francisco, Boston, Atlanta, Los Angeles, and Toronto.

Besides the usual resources of the social scientist, I have also been assisted in the present undertaking by the fact that I myself am a transplanted American from China. In work, play, and raising a family I have shared the advantages and disadvantages, the hopes and despairs, of all Chinese–Americans. To that extent I am hopeful that this book will convey to the reader something of the personal reactions, feelings, and insights of at least one of the subjects of the study.

I am indebted to a number of friends and scholars whose comments on the manuscript, in whole or in part, have been of great help. For this I wish to thank Professor and Mrs. Kenneth A. Abbott, Sacramento State College, Mara Brownson, Wadsworth Publishing Company, Dr. Walter Char and Dr. Donald Char, University of Hawaii, Mrs. Clarence Chang, Mr. Lowell Chun-Hoon, Yale University, Professor Alexander DeConde, University of California, Santa Barbara, Joan Gordon, Encyclopedia Britannica Educational Corporation, Mr. Chinn Ho, Professor and Mrs. John Israel, University of Virginia, Reverend Harold Jow, United Church of Christ, Honolulu, Professor Daniel Kwok, University of Hawaii, and Mr. Edwin Yee, Holiday Mart, Hawaii. Of course, I alone am responsible for its defects.

The research that went into this book is part of a larger continuing study from 1949 to 1970 under the auspices of the Wenner–Gren Foundation for anthropological Research. At its inception I was also helped by a grant from the Social Science Research Council.

The first two drafts of the manuscript were written while I was associated with the East–West Center and the Department of American Studies at the University of Hawaii. Miss Cynthia Ai at the University of Hawaii, and my daughter, Penny, separately edited them for style, grammar, and often content. The kind and efficient ladies of the Center's typing pool, under the direction of Mrs. Hazel Tatsuno (who never allowed her larger responsibilities as Executive Secretary of the Center's Institute of Advanced Projects to prevent her from her care for details) did the rest. The final chores before going to press fell on the shoulders of Mrs. Adele Andelson, who has ably assisted me at Northwestern University for many years.

Francis L. K. Hsu

CONTENTS

ONE   Different Kinds of Chinese   1

TWO   The Chinese Language   11

THREE   Family and Kinship   19

FOUR   Family Behavior and the American Context   29

FIVE   The Attraction of Local Ties   39

SIX   Religion   53

SEVEN   Friendship and Hospitality   67

EIGHT   Adolescence   83

NINE   Prejudice   95

TEN   Americanization and the American Dream   111

ELEVEN   Chinese Identity and the American Dream   123

APPENDIX   The Human Equation in Our Future   137

Recommended Reading   153

Index   157

THE CHALLENGE OF THE AMERICAN DREAM:

The Chinese in the United States

Mrs. Woo Yao-tsu, Ph.D. in chemistry (left), chats with a friend in her California Institute of Technology laboratory.

Chapter One

Different Kinds
of Chinese

The old Western image of the Chinese dies hard.

In the 20's and 30's, bearded or unbearded Shylock-like Jews supplied most of the minority-joke material for movies, radio, comics, and cartoons. Then the Jews organized themselves through the Anti-Defamation League and other systematic efforts. Now the only public amusement at the expense of Jews is supplied by Jews themselves, for themselves.

In the 40's, 50's and even part of the 60's, Negro stereotypes—especially the happy-go-lucky and Uncle Tom types—were much in evidence in comics, movies, radio, and later television programs. But now the Negroes have organized and arisen. It is impossible to watch television for any length of time without seeing Negroes (now called Blacks) in all types of commercials and programs in the roles of heroes and heroines. Blacks have made the big time in the movies. Sidney Poitier commands a star's salary, acting only in roles which portray him as the hero.

The Chinese, however, still fare as badly in the public media as they have in the past. Their best parts in movies are still as shady characters, servants, laundrymen, or spies speaking broken English, with pigtails on the back of their heads, and a silly grin on their otherwise expressionless faces, bowing every step of the way and being the victims in any sort of quarrel. The best parts for Chinese women stagnate at the level of being exotic, mysterious, or submissive. On the rare occasions in which a Chinese is featured in a role of some importance, the real facts about the Chinese are so mixed up that they are on a level with *Alice in Wonderland.* The Chinese wife of the Irish hero in a

1967 television Western was totally incapacitated by her bound feet. She was seen being carried around until she died in an accident. The movie, "Thoroughly Modern Millie," shown throughout the nation in 1968, uses every American device for demeaning the Chinese. The Chinese in that movie are opium-smoking white slavers and cowards to boot. They are continually bested by the white, gangster-like woman proprietor of a questionable hotel. This woman is supposed to converse with them in Chinese, but her Chinese consisted of no more than garbled syllables which sounded for the most part like the hissing of cats.[1]

In spite of the fact that Chinese language and culture programs have sprung up in many American universities, colleges, and even in some high schools, the ignorance concerning the Chinese language and culture is appalling. The worst of it is that there does not seem to be any desire on the part of the American public to learn the truth. Last Christmas a friend sent me a beautiful card made from a steel engraving of a Canton street scene by a member of a so-called British Expedition to China in 1843–1844. The portrayal of the Chinese street is delightful and faithful except that not one of the legible Chinese characters on the many shop signs is Chinese. The supposedly Chinese characters are no more than clusters of vertical, horizontal, or curly lines which the artist, ignorant of Chinese calligraphy, had fabricated without taking the trouble to consult an expert. After more than a century of contact, the American portrayal of things Chinese—in comics, in cartoons, and even in artistically valuable paintings—has undergone no change where the Chinese language is concerned. It continues to be depicted with meaningless clusters of vertical, horizontal, or curly lines.

There are, in general, four identifiable groups of Chinese in America: (1) Chinatown-centered Chinese; (2) Chinese in Hawaii; (3) scholars and professionals, a majority of whom had at least part of their higher education in China and settled in the United States since World War II; and (4) college students from China, industrial, business, and military trainees from China, visiting merchants, and governmental representatives.

Of course, these groupings are not absolute. Many of the Chinatown-centered Chinese who succeed financially reside in or move to other parts of the cities or suburban areas and visit Chinatowns infrequently, albeit the latter may still have symbolic value for them. This is true of the Chinese in San Francisco and Los Angeles no less than of Sacramento, Boston, Detroit, Chicago, and New York. Some of them, including immigrants and their American-born descendants of the second, third, and fourth generations, are big businessmen and professionals. In view of the remarkably high number of Chinese–Americans who have finished college and graduate school since the mid-40's, it is obvious that, in time, even more of them will gravitate away from Chinatowns.

Many scholars and professionals who do not live in Chinatowns have more contact there than grocery shopping or restaurant sampling. They may help organize certain projects and some of their children may participate in

Chinatown's beauty contests and other public events. Some of them have studied Chinatowns or some aspect of Chinese life in America. Many of them have been asked by their white friends or colleagues to serve as unofficial guides to Chinatowns or Chinese restaurants. Whether they have these additional contacts or not, if they are anywhere near a Chinatown, Whites will presume some inside knowledge on their part; it is difficult for them to profess ignorance under the circumstances.

Those who came as students may decide to stay after completion of their education. In that case, they move from the fourth group to the second or third, depending upon how they develop their careers. The same process may occur in the case of business or governmental representatives. Some have become editors of Chinatown papers or executives of Chinatown-connected civic organizations. One of the highest officials of the Kuomintang retired on Long Island, where he ran a chicken farm for some time. I know at least two plush Chinese restaurants, one in New York and one in Washington, D.C., which are owned and operated by former high Chinese officials. Other former members of the Chinese diplomatic corps now work as company employees, engineers, salesmen, and professors. Dr. Ta-chung Liu, a distinguished professor of economics at Cornell University, was formerly the Economic Attaché of the Chinese Embassy in Washington, D.C.

Two points should be made clear at once. On the one hand, a great deal of diversity exists within each of these groups. For example, some Chinese scholars have little in common with Chinese professionals such as bankers or real estate brokers. The contrast between those who cling to the relative state of squalor and disrepair in the area still called Honolulu's Chinatown and the occupants of the numerous palatial residences of the Chinese in Hawaii is not unlike that between Appalachian Whites and Beverley Hills celebrities. Sharp contrasts obtain even among the highly successful. For example, there are Chinese businessmen in Hawaii of considerable means who are active participants in Chinatown-connected organizations. Their calling cards indicate that they are present or past presidents of numerous such organizations. But Chinn Ho, developer of Makaha Valley, whose portrait has been featured on the covers of *Money,* a Wall Street journal, and other publications, has practically no connection with them at all.

On the other hand, there is little confusion in the minds of the average Chinese as to who belongs to which group. For example, the common Chinese term for Chinese born in the United States is *t'u sheng.* This term is used frequently in conversation. But it is rarely used to designate children born in the United States of Chinese parents who came as scholars, professionals, or students. Another example is found on college campuses across the country. American-born Chinese students rarely get together with those who came from Taiwan or Hongkong. This is true in Ivy League schools no less than in others. Consequently, U.S.-born Chinese college students, as their numbers increase, may in time form a group distinct from their forebears and from college students coming from Taiwan, Hongkong, and mainland China.

The Chinatown-Centered Chinese

Chinatown-centered Chinese are either descendants of ancestors who came from Kwangtung province (of which Kwangchow is the capital) or former inhabitants of that province. They are known as Cantonese because Kwangtung is pronounced Canton according to the dialect of the province. The first Cantonese to come to the United States were merchants. But the bulk of Cantonese who followed them were laborers, as were nearly all immigrant ethnic groups in the nineteenth century. The Chinese laborers came in the second half of that century for the California Gold Rush and later played a crucial role in the race between the Central Pacific and the Union Pacific Railroads in extending their respective lines until they met. Central Pacific imported about 14,000 Chinese and won the race by pushing the line 1,000 miles inland across such forbidding barriers as the bitter cold of Donner Pass and the withering heat of the Nevada desert. They also played an important role in agricultural development throughout the West.

However, even during the Gold Rush, white brutality and outright bandit-like behavior robbed many Chinese claimstakers and mining prospectors of their gains. To insure a livelihood, many Chinese became traders or settled for performing services, such as doing laundry, for the white miners. After the railroad was completed, most of the early miners and laborers returned to China. Those who stayed were, for the most part, professionals, skilled workers, merchants, and those laborers who could move up into these occupational categories. They became the ancestors of the fourth-, fifth-, and sixth-generation Cantonese–Americans. From a few restricted localities on the West Coast they then dispersed to many parts of the United States, including Los Angeles, Seattle, Phoenix, Detroit, Chicago, New York City, New England, and even the South.

The Chinese in Hawaii

A majority of the Hawaiian Chinese forebears came as plantation laborers, a few came as tradesmen to serve the plantation Chinese, and a still smaller number came as preachers, teachers of the Chinese language, and doctors. They, too, came from Kwangtung province and are known as Cantonese. Their only difference in origin is that, whereas about 80 percent of the United States mainland Chinatown-centered Chinese trace their origin to Ssu Yi, a four-district area of Kwangtung, the immigrants to Hawaii came from Chung Shan, a district adjacent to the four.

The early Chinese who came to mainland United States came without families. The traditional Chinese pattern was for men searching for a livelihood temporarily to leave their families at home. However, when circumstances changed and they wanted to bring their families from China, they were prevented from doing so, before World War II, by the United States government's exclusionist policies, supported by the hostile white environment of California and elsewhere. Some intermarriage with non-Chinese occurred, but not frequently. Consequently, immigrants clustered in bachelor dormitories or rooming houses in Chinatowns, a situation highly conducive to gambling and other vices. The financially able returned to China to buy land, marry, or reunite with their families periodically. In 1860 the sex ratio among the Chinese in mainland United States was 100 females to 1,859 males. The situation actually worsened somewhat in the next 40 years; by 1900, this ratio was 100 to 1,887.[2] Thereafter, it became less disproportionate and the female-to-male ratio came to 100:695 in 1920 and 100:135 in 1960.

By contrast, the sex ratio among the Chinese in Hawaii has always been less disproportionate. The early Chinese immigrants to Hawaii also came with few women.[3] But soon they married Hawaiian women, who were not averse to interracial unions. By 1920 there was still a marked excess of males over females in the forty and older age groups while the sex ratio among younger age groups had approached normal. By 1960 the Chinese sex ratio in Hawaii was normal for all age groups.

Long before I first visited Hawaii in 1949, I had been told by both Chinese and Whites that the Chinese in Hawaii were unlike those in mainland United States. While the Chinese and non-Chinese speakers might have had different meanings in mind, a number of facts are obvious. For one thing, even in 1949 men of Chinese ancestry were prominent in Hawaii's political, professional, and business ranks; today, that prominence has become greatly augmented. One example of this is that it was Chinese enterprise which first broke into the Big Five's control of transportation by establishing Aloha Airlines (formerly Trans-Pacific Airline) to compete with Hawaiian Airlines. Also, the Chinese residential pattern became dispersed quite early. Whites for many years did maintain exclusive areas such as Pacific Heights, the ocean side of Kahala Avenue, and the upper levels of Manoa Valley. But today it is difficult to find a favored section of Honolulu without some Chinese inhabitants. The so-called Chinatown in Honolulu contains only a tiny fraction of the Chinese population and their businesses. Most Chinese of Hawaii today have long left it, or have had little or nothing to do with it. The Narcissus Festival, the highlight of which is the crowning of a Queen, is perhaps the largest Chinese annual event sponsored by the United Chinese Benevolent Association and the Chinese Chamber of Commerce. But it is no more than a carnival where people have a good time; there is no interchange of ideas. Hawaii's Chinatown is at present being rebuilt under a new plan by some energetic Chinese business interests. But it is unlikely to be of importance for most of Hawaii's Chinese, either economically or symbolically.

Two other features also distinguish Hawaii's Chinese from most Chinese in the other states. In the period 1960–1964, over half of the Chinese marriages in Hawaii involved a non-Chinese spouse. To be sure, the social atmosphere of Hawaii has always favored intermarriage, beginning with the Hawaiians themselves. But not all ethnic groups in Hawaii have practiced it to the same extent. The lowest outmarriage rate in the years named above was found among the Japanese (15.7 percent), while the Chinese rate (54.8 percent) was topped by those of Puerto Ricans (65.0 percent), Koreans (77.1 percent), and, of course, the Hawaiians (85.9 percent).[4] The other distinguishing feature concerns education. In 1910 only a little over half (57.3 percent) of Chinese 16- and 17-year-olds were attending school. By 1950 the Chinese of that age group had the highest high school attendance rate (94.1 percent), equalled only by Hawaii's Japanese, followed by Filipinos (81.1 percent), Hawaiians and part-Hawaiians (78.1 percent), and Caucasians (77.4 percent).[5]

Scholars and Professionals

Not long ago, a widely circulated magazine featured an article praising the spectacular progress of the Chinese in America. The gist of the article is that the Chinese, from illiterate and penniless laboring origins, were able to produce two Nobel Prize winners in a few generations. From laundryman to Nobel Prize winner is indeed a spectacular jump. But had the writer looked a little beneath the surface he would have realized that the Chinese Nobel Prize winners were not only born and raised in mainland China, but also that they had earned their bachelor's degrees from a Chinese university (a wartime makeshift university, at that!) before they came to the United States for graduate work.

The fact is, nearly all Chinese scholars and most Chinese professionals in America today were born, raised, and educated to the bachelor-degree level in mainland China or Taiwan. This is true no less of the Chinese Nobel Prize winners than of Ch'ien Hsueh-shen, the Chinese jet-propulsion expert, one-time professor at MIT and California Tech, and currently a most important figure in mainland China's atomic and rocketry programs.

A look at the roster of Chinese professors in American universities or at *American Men of Science* will leave no doubt on this point. Some mainland American-born Chinese have achieved fame in the arts and professions: James Wong Howe, cinematographer; Dong Kingman, watercolorist; Robert Lee, church affairs; Worley K. Wong, architect; and Chin Y. Lee, author of *Flower Drum Song*. But most well-known Chinese in the United States came from China as adults: the Wall Street wizard, Gerald Ts'ai, head of the Manhattan Mutual Fund and other enterprises (though Ts'ai obtained his bachelor's degree in the United States), and world-famous architect, I. M. Pei.

As we mentioned above, the Chinatown-centered Chinese and Hawaii's Chinese are of Kwangtung origin and are generally known as Cantonese. But Chinese scholars and professionals are, in addition to being first-generation immigrants, usually from Northern, Central, and Eastern provinces of China, including Kiangsu, Chekiang, Shantung, Hupei, and Hopei. Their native tongues are non-Cantonese and they are usually able to understand or command some sort of Mandarin—the standard northern Chinese dialect adopted as the lingua franca in mainland China for 50 years and in Taiwan since World War II.

Another characteristic of this group is that they have little or no connection with Chinatown-centered organizations, such as "The Six Companies" rooted in San Francisco or the community-based organizations such as Chung Shan T'ung Hsiang Hui (Chung Shan Community Association) of Honolulu. Instead, they have much more to do with non-Chinese nationwide professional or social groups (such as the American Medical Association and the Rotary International) or local interest groups (such as the PTA or neighborhood improvement associations). There are some loosely organized, purely Chinese associations among them; one of these is the Midwest Chinese Student and Alumnus Services.

Finally, Chinese of this group are to be found in every state of the Union. Their office mates, colleagues, and neighbors are generally non-Chinese. If they need help they are likely to go to the usual employment agencies, social work agencies, banks, and research foundations run and patronized mostly by Whites.

The Transients

I call the fourth group transients—consisting of college students from China, visiting merchants, industrial business and military trainees, and governmental representatives—because that is their most obvious characteristic. The trainees stay as little as a few weeks to a few months. The students, merchants, and governmental representatives remain somewhat longer, from one to several years. Some of them may later become permanent residents and citizens, but in the normal course of events they depart in less than five years.[6]

Like the scholars and professionals, members of this group come from all parts of China and generally speak Mandarin Chinese with some fluency, even if they came from Hongkong or Taiwan. Many of the governmental representatives come with their wives and children, but most of the students and nearly all trainees do not. Many of the students work part time or during vacations in Chinese restaurants in Chinatowns and elsewhere. But, increasingly, they also find vacation work in businesses and factories. They live in dormitories, rooming houses, and the homes of temporary foster parents arranged by such organizations as the Friends of East–West Center in Hawaii and church organizations elsewhere.

According to a 1970 report, there are at present 16,230 Chinese students in American colleges and universities. California tops the list with about 3,000, while Alaska has only 5, the smallest number. The distribution by institution is shown in Table 1.

Table 1

Number and Institution	Number of Chinese Students
1 Berkeley	over 500
5 Illinois, Minnesota, Wisconsin, New York, U.C.L.A.	over 200
20 Stanford, Southern California, San Francisco State, St. Louis, Hawaii, Southern Illinois, Indiana, Purdue, Kansas State, Harvard, Massachusetts, M.I.T., Michigan, Columbia, Cornell, Oklahoma State, Oregon, Pennsylvania, Tennessee, Washington	
	over 100
85	over 50
98	over 20

Source: Office of Cultural Affairs of the Chinese Embassy, Washington, D.C., as reported in *Chung Yang Jih Pao* (*Central Daily News*), Taipei, Taiwan, Sept. 2, 1970.

General Observations

Of the four groups, the Chinatown-centered one is by far the largest. According to the latest United States Census, it is about 400,000. Hawaii has about 38,000 persons of Chinese ancestry, who form between 5 to 6 percent of the population in the Islands. The transient group is the third, numbering about 18,000.[7] The scholar and professional group comes last, with probably between 5,000 and 6,000 members at this writing.[8]

Previously we noted that the demarcation lines of the four groups were not absolute. The ancestors of Chinatown-centered Chinese were drawn from landless laborers in Kwangtung province, in contrast to Chinese in the last two groups drawn primarily from more well-to-do families of scholars and high officials. It is only natural that, thus far, vertical mobility among the Chinatown-centered Chinese has been numerically insignificant. They had to do it the hard way; they were least prepared by their background and suffered the brunt of white American prejudice. Even the second- and third-generation Chinese in Hawaii, many of whom have achieved social positions undreamed of by their forefathers, look primarily to business, medicine, dentistry, and law as the sources of their success. By contrast, most of the scholars and professionals, having been imbued with the literary culture of China, tend to be intellectually oriented. Even as engineers, they mostly teach or do research in universities and industry. As of this writing, most of the Chinese faculty members of even the University of Hawaii were born and raised in mainland China or Taiwan.

There is, of course, nothing permanent about this picture. Indications are that, as the generations roll on, we can reasonably expect more American-born Chinese to find their way into the universities. In the words of Dr. Donald Char, a third-generation Hawaiian-born Chinese, "Our achievements in medicine and law, rather than letters and humanities, I would like to think, are due partly to our pragmatic backgrounds. Traditionally, rewards within the American system but outside of these fields seem much less promising. In addition, there were few models for us to emulate within the structure of higher education at the time we were growing up, which accounts for my feeling that we must develop respected status in the educational hierarchy if we are to have some members of our younger generation succeed us in this area." [9]

Those Chinese students forced by circumstances to find Chinatown-connected work on a part-time basis or during vacations tend to have but a temporary association with the Chinatown-centered Chinese. But the governmental representatives (from mainland China before 1949 and from Taiwan since then) have as their principal responsibility to work with the Chinatown-centered and Hawaiian Chinese. These are what the Chinese government has traditionally termed *hwa ch'iao* or overseas chinese. Such representatives are always invited to give ceremonial speeches at all major Chinatown functions and other affairs of community or clan associations. When General Ts'ai T'ing Kai, famous for his brilliant battles against superior-equipped invading Japanese forces near Shanghai in 1932, toured the United States, his tumultuous welcome and magnificent receptions were organized and underwritten by Chinatowns or Chinatown-connected organizations throughout the country.

To conclude this review we need to say something about a group which consisted of what the late sociologist, Dr. Rose Hum Lee—one of the few scholars rising from among the Chinatown-centered Chinese[10]—called "stranded Chinese." [11] These Chinese students came to the United States between the end of World War II and the ascension of Communist power in China in 1949. By the normal process of education many of them would have been ready to return to their homeland from 1950 onwards. The number who were thus stranded was estimated to be somewhere around 1,500.

Most Whites see America as such a golden land of opportunity that they find it impossible to think of anyone unhappy about being stranded here. But from the Chinese point of view the matter is not so simple. To begin with, under the generally discriminatory attitude of Whites, many of these highly trained Chinese (most with master's and doctoral degrees) had up to that time to settle for positions much below that to which their training would have entitled them. Even more basic, most Chinese never had the idea of settling outside of China once their education was completed. This is a point to which we shall return in a later chapter. For the moment we must note that, in spite of the political change of 1949, a number of Chinese students returned to mainland China; others voluntarily chose to remain in the United States or were compelled by the American government to do so.

In 1950 a group of some 30 Chinese students en route to China was turned back at Honolulu. Their exit permits were perfectly in order but our government had a sudden change of mind. After the outbreak of the Korean War in that year, most Chinese students, especially in the engineering and physical sciences, were expressly forbidden to leave the country. This was the beginning of the persecution and house detention of Ch'ien Hsueh-shen, the jet-propulsion expert we mentioned earlier.

However, America is a land of opportunity even for those whose forebears she once excluded. The stranded Chinese students soon made realistic adjustments. By the 1960's most of them had joined the ranks of scholars and professionals.

Notes

1. The Chinese characters fare better in a few other movies such as "The Love Bug" (a Disney film which includes a completely delightful scene with Buddy Hackett speaking credible Cantonese), "Alice's Restaurant" (in which Arlo Guthrie's girl is a Chinese lab technician), and "True Grit" (in which John Wayne has a Chinese friend). I have not seen these films and am indebted to Mrs. John Israel for bringing them to my attention.

2. The sex ratio among those of marriageable age between 20 and 50 was not so lopsided but nonetheless very disproportionate.

3. In 1865, when the Chinese population in Hawaii numbered about 1,300, 52 wives came to join them (see George C. Hull, "Chinese in Hawaii," *Mid-Pacific Magazine,* March 1917).

4. Andrew Lind, *Hawaii's People,* Honolulu, University of Hawaii Press, 1967, p. 110.

5. *Ibid.,* p. 91.

6. During the two decades following World War II, a large proportion of Chinese students in the United States turned into permanent immigrants. However, rising unemployment, especially among the highly educated, in the late sixties, has since altered the picture considerably.

7. 16,230 are students. Office of Cultural Affairs of the Chinese Embassy, Washington, D.C., as reported in *Chung Yang Jih Pao (Central Daily News),* Taipei, Taiwan, Sept. 2, 1970.

8. 3,117 are university faculty members and administrators *(ibid.).*

9. Personal communication. Dr. Char is a physician, Director of Student Health and Professor of Public Health at the University of Hawaii.

10. She was born in Montana of parents who kept a small store.

11. "The Stranded Chinese in the United States," *Phylon* 19, No. 2 (Summer 1958), 180–194.

Mrs. Shih Chao-Ying and her late husband, who was Nationalist Chinese Consul-General at Ottawa and later Nationalist Chinese Ambassador to Brazil. (Photo by Yusef Karsh.)

Chapter Two

The Chinese Language

Chinese is by no means an easy language, but its difficulties have been exaggerated, especially in a number of popular misconceptions.

I have often been asked, "How do Chinese talk to each other since they cannot understand each other's language?" In the warlord years (1911–1928) some observers of China claimed that one reason for so much internal strife was that there were so many dialect groups which could not communicate with each other. Another notion current among many non-Chinese is that Chinese is very hard to master and, in fact, is the most difficult language in the world. Quite a few American students who are interested in the Far East have avoided China expressly because the language, they believe, is so difficult to learn.

The Dialects

The idea that Chinese from different parts of the country cannot talk to each other is baseless. Perhaps my own experiences will help to illustrate its absurdity. I was born in a small village in South Manchuria. When I was six years old we moved from that village to a small town in Western Manchuria about 500 miles away. The dialect at my command when I entered school was different from that of most of my classmates and they made my life miserable by deriding me as a dumb outsider. But they and I understood each other without any difficulty. In less than six weeks I mastered their dialect although I continued to speak my mother dialect at home.

Later my father sent me to high school in the big North China city,

T'ientsin, in Hopei province. There the local people spoke a dialect different from the two I already knew. Again it was the same story. They and I understood each other perfectly, and in less than a month I added the T'ientsin dialect to my linguistic repertoire.

Still later, during World War II, I met my wife in Yunnan province, part of what then was known as Free China. My wife was born in Central China and she spoke (and still does) the Hankow variety of the Hupei (province) dialect. The reader will gain some idea of the distances involved by thinking of the place of my birth as Canton, Maine; the place where I attended grade school as Hanover, Vermont; the place where I attended high school as Albany, New York; the place where my wife was born as St. Louis, Missouri, and the place where we met as Dallas, Texas. With practically no linguistic adjustment at all, I had little trouble lecturing to my Yunnan-raised students or understanding my Hankow-born wife.

What I have said about these widely separated areas holds equally true of North Central and Northwest China. The fact is that, except for the southeastern coastal belt extending from approximately Shanghai to Canton, all Chinese speak dialects that vary more or less from Mandarin, known as *kuo yü* or national speech. An average Chinese can usually tell a Yunnanese speaker from another who hails from Hupei, and the latter from one from the Northwest, for example Kansu. Their linguistic differences are, however, hardly greater than those which separate natives of Brooklyn, New York, Chicago, and Los Angeles.

On the other hand, the differences which separate the six dialects from Shanghai to Canton are much greater. A Northern Chinese cannot make himself easily understood in Shanghai, Foochow, or Canton. The other three main dialects in this coastal belt are Northern Chekiang, Southern Chekiang and Amoy or Swatow. When I went to the University of Shanghai as a freshman, I came upon the first true language barrier in my life. I simply could not understand the people I met nor they me. Later I was to have the same experience in Canton. However, in three months I comprehended the Shanghai dialect. Six months later I conversed in it with a fluency adequate for most purposes; I was no longer conspicuous.

I am not a linguistic genius, though I admit to being somewhat gifted in that regard; it took me much, much longer to master English and I am still unable to claim a comparable degree of fluency in French and Japanese after laboring in the former for three years and the latter for one year. The reason I was able to master the Shanghai dialect so quickly is that no grammatical differences separate any of the Chinese dialects—the mutually intelligible ones as well as the mutually unintelligible ones. Their differences are primarily phonetic ones, with only marginal dissimilarities in idiom.[1]

Mandarin

Mandarin has often been referred to, erroneously, by Chinese and non-Chinese alike, as Peking dialect. What they should have used instead is the term *kuo yü* (national speech), which is a more correct translation of the term Mandarin. Since *kuo yü* is closer to Peking dialect and since Peking traditionally has been and in modern times is the nation's capital, most people have identified the one with the other. Pure Peking dialect has many phonetic peculiarities not found in Mandarin Chinese.

Just when Mandarin was first proclaimed to be the national speech is not clear. No such proclamation was made before the fall of the Manchu dynasty in 1911. On the other hand, the greatest impetus for its national popularity certainly came from the "May 4th Chinese Renaissance Movement" of 1919 led by Dr. Hu Shih. Since the 1920's, but especially since the firm establishment of the Nationalist government under Generalissimo Chiang Kai-shek, the supremacy of Mandarin became unquestioned. It was taught in all public and private schools and also became known as *p'u t'ung hua* or common speech.

By the 1930's this common speech was in general circulation in all cities and achieved no small degree of acceptance in small towns. Even in villages in the southeastern coastal belt between Shanghai and Canton, where the dialects are markedly different from each other and from those of the rest of the country, Mandarin speakers were not rare. The late Professor Ta Ch'en, a sociologist of the National Ts'ing Hua University of Peking, related in the early 30's his experiences in interior Fukien province, the mainland province situated across the sea from Taiwan. At one point he and his assistants were lost. From one of the homes to which they went for help came a boy of 12 or 13 who used excellent Mandarin to direct them out of their predicament.

Today, throughout mainland China and Taiwan, Mandarin is the speech which will be understood everywhere. Its rapid spread in Taiwan is remarkable indeed. Up to 1945, when Japan surrendered the island to China, most Taiwanese spoke only the native tongue of their Southern Fukien origin. Those who were bilingual had Japanese as their second language since that was the language enforced in the schools for half a century. But by 1961, when I last visited the island, a majority of the Taiwanese of 30 years or less understood and spoke Mandarin with some degree of proficiency—although the old dialect has not faded away.

A principal reason for the rapid spread of Mandarin is, as we noted before, that basically most Chinese dialects vary so little from it. Another reason is that even dialects which possess drastically different phonetic traits that make them unintelligible to the other Chinese share the same grammar. This is one reason why even speakers of Cantonese and Fukienese did not oppose the spread of Mandarin.[2] In view of the enormous and irreconcilable problems presented by the many opposing linguistic groups in India, which keep that country divided and tend to be used as reason for further division, the Chinese lack of such opposition is remarkable indeed. The different Chinese dialect groups, while maintaining their mother tongues, offered no opposition to the spread of Mandarin in spite of the fact that China was not free from regional rivalries and strife on other issues.

Of course not all Chinese of different regions command Mandarin with equal facility even when they speak it. When a group of Chinese get together, one of the conversational diversions consists of mutual attempts to pinpoint a person's native province through an analysis of his speech. One person may assert that another is from Szechuan because "I can tell from his speech," or "I cannot believe you are from the South because your Mandarin is so perfect," and so on. There are inevitably some comments that are not complimentary, such as the following Northern (naturally) Chinese jingle indicates:

> I can laugh at God's fury,
> The earth I can master;
> But a Mandarin-speaking Cantonese,
> Is too great a disaster.

The Literary Chinese

For over 3,000 years the Chinese written language remained separate from speech. To be sure, until modern times not more than five or ten percent of the males could read and write. But those who could dealt with a written language that bore little resemblance to any of the spoken dialects. Even without prior knowledge of Chinese, the reader will be able to appreciate the distance between written and spoken Chinese from the following phonetic transcriptions of a passage of Confucian Analects, first in its original and then in Mandarin:

1. *Tsu yueh: Hsueh er shih hsi tzu, pu yi yueh hu?*
2. *Lao shih shuo: Nian shu huan neng ch'ang ch'ang wen hsi t'a, na pu shih k'uai le ma?* Translation—the Master said: "To learn and to be able to practice what one learns, does that not make one happy?"

The Chinese written language has no set alphabet like English or set syllables like Hindi. Instead it consists of many characters, each of which is a little ideograph, distinct and recognizable. So, traditionally, linguists have called the Chinese language monosyllabic, in contrast to polysyllabic European languages. In recent years this view has been under attack. The opponents note that, when we take the spoken Chinese into consideration, many Chinese usages are in fact polysyllabic. For example, in Chinese speech the expression *"tung hsi"* stands for "things," as in "what things do you have there?" Separately, the word *"tung"* means "east," and *"hsi"* means "west." It is only when they are combined that they bear the meaning "things."

Then there are arguments on the merits or the demerits of the Chinese written language. One is that its peculiar structure prevented the development of science. An effective reply to this argument is found in the monumental works of Professor Joseph Needham of Cambridge University, entitled *Science and Civilisation in China.*[3] Needham shows that the Chinese achieved an enormous amount of scientific know-how, both theoretical and practical, generally in advance of Westerners. Whatever was responsible for the lag of Chinese science during the last three hundred years, the Chinese language cannot be blamed.

Another alleged demerit of the Chinese written language is that, by being so different from its spoken counterpart, it prevented the spread of literacy. But the nature of the Chinese traditional social structure defined literacy as the privilege of the few. And no Chinese government before contact with the West had ever intended that all Chinese read and write, even as a remote possibility.

Against these alleged demerits, there are several points in its favor. For example, the fact that the written and spoken languages are separate has enabled literary Chinese to serve as unifiers throughout China. A literate Northern Chinese in Kwangtung and a literate Fukienese in Peking could at least use an intrinsically Chinese medium for communication—and not some foreign tongue, as many peoples have to do in India, Africa, and Europe under similar circumstances. Even most Japanese, whose language has an enormously different grammatical structure and who have adopted written Chinese since the 7th century A.D., can usually communicate with the average Chinese today in writing. This, in my view, was another reason why Chinese in different parts of the country, with their own distinct dialects, did not oppose the spread of Mandarin.

The modern American reader who has taken a look at Chaucerian English will readily concede that he cannot read it at all, and Chaucerian English is only about five centuries old. By contrast a modern Chinese educated reader has little difficulty in understanding the works of the historian, Ssu-ma Ch'ien, who wrote in the 1st century A.D. In fact, without special effort, he can also read a good many of the characters inscribed on the pre-historical oracle bones uncovered in North China dated about 1700 B.C.

Thus, the fact is that written English has changed much more in a shorter time than has written Chinese over a much longer period of time. Written Chinese has been able to remain more constant, in part because it was not as closely related to spoken Chinese. This lack of major change has enabled the Chinese to have a greater sense of identification with their past. It diminishes their desire for change, and it has also buttressed the feeling of unity between the generations. It was another factor which indirectly helped the rapid spread of Mandarin as the lingua franca of China.

The Vernacular

Even before modern times, not all written matter was in literary Chinese. Some of the best novels since the Yuan dynasty (1260–1380 A.D.) were written in a vernacular, that is, the spoken language. The *Odes* and some poetry dating back to much earlier times also incorporated elements of the vernacular. Often there is a mixture of the two, but the use of the spoken language is unmistakable. However, the use of the vernacular as a desired form of written medium did not begin until Dr. Hu Shih launched the Chinese Renaissance Movement in 1919. The terms *pai hua* (the vernacular) as distinguished from *wen yen* (literary Chinese) have been used since that time.

The Chinese Renaissance Movement was against many traditional usages and ideas including funeral customs, marital practices, filial piety, Taoist magic and beliefs, and most of Confucianism. But the singular and most important result of this movement was the legitimization of the Mandarin-based vernacular throughout China. The success of the vernacular as a generally accepted public and private medium, in turn, gave further impetus to the spread of Mandarin as the *p'u t'ung hua* of China.

There was some opposition from the older generations of scholars. Some of them considered the vernacular to be a degenerate form of the Chinese language. Others thought the spread of the vernacular would diminish the beauty of the Chinese language. The warlords in their internecine warfare always made their proclamations and denouncements in a style Confucius would have approved. Dr. Sun Yat-sen's last will, which became the central part of any public meeting under the Nationalist government, was written in literary Chinese and read aloud accordingly. Even the public pronouncements of the Nationalist government at Nanking after it unified all China were, as a rule, in the traditional literary style. In the minds of many older Chinese, the use of vernacular even in personal correspondence was equated to a confession of a lack of proper education.

However, vernacular publications mushroomed everywhere. Energetic and talented writers edited magazines and wrote novels only in the vernacular. In this the pens of Lu Hsun, Kuo Mo-jo, Hsu Chih-mo, and Pa Chin were among the most powerful. Some of the most popular literary contests were conducted in the vernacular. In addition, nearly all young people in schools and colleges corresponded with each other in the vernacular. Writing in the vernacular soon became an accepted practice rather than a matter of literary embarrassment. An alphabet was constructed, not to replace the characters but to aid in reading and learning. There was also a "One Thousand Character" movement which aimed to restrict the number of characters to be used, in the same manner that the designers of Basic English tried to limit English to some 860 nouns and 160 verbs, adjectives, conjunctions, and articles. Neither of these devices lasted, but the vernacular is here to stay.

Yet, true to the Chinese way of doing things, a way which we shall elaborate on in subsequent chapters, *wen yen* (literary Chinese) did not die out. Rather it coexisted with *pai hua* (the vernacular), just as the spread of *kuo yü* did not drive out the dialects. Students corresponded with their peers in the vernacular but wrote letters home to their parents in the literary style. Public and official documents, including those for marriages, divorces, and obituaries, continued to be in the literary style, but newspaper writing tended to be mixed, with editorials more *wen yen* than *pai hua* but other departments more *pai hua* than *wen yen*.

The long-term trend will be, of course, for *pai hua* to expand at the expense of *wen yen*. This has been evident in mainland China since 1949. There, even the dialogues in the national Chinese opera (popularly called "Peking Opera"), which used to be mostly in *wen yen*, full of literary allusions, have been changed over to *pai hua*. There, too, simplified Chinese characters have gained greater acceptance than ever before.

Written Language among the Chinese in America

Since transients, scholars, and professionals came to the United States with some degree of knowledge of *wen yen* and *pai hua*, they tend to be like the educated Chinese in China. Insofar as they use Chinese at all, they use one or the other as the occasion requires. As some of the transients enter the scholar and professional group, and as the latter group continues living and working in the United States, they will have more and more occasion to use English with the result that their skill in written Chinese will necessarily suffer. A minority of Chinese scholars in the United States has written articles and a few books in Chinese, publishing them in Taiwan or Hongkong; most have written in English and published in this country.

But the Chinese written language continues to be of importance among the Chinatown-centered Chinese in mainland United States and even among many of the Chinese in Hawaii. Since these two groups generally were not the descendants of educated men and women, the written Chinese they use tends, in the first place, to be business-connected. In China it has always been recognized that traders and craftsmen traditionally kept accounts and communicated with each other in a sort of semiliterate written Chinese. It has terms and set phrases of its own, comparable to the literary allusions in *wen yen*, but they are not true literary allusions because they have no basis in the well-known writings of the ancients.

As they or their children become more affluent and rise on the social ladder, the Chinese written language they use is more likely to be *wen yen* than *pai hua*. This is especially true where ritual and ceremonial functions are concerned. Tombstones often are inscribed in Chinese as well as English. The Chinese inscription is invariably in *wen yen*. Those who worship at Chinese temples often petition the gods in *wen yen*. Chinese restaurants and shops usually have on their walls and doors felicitous sentiments written on red or gold papers, invariably expressed in *wen yen*.

Such usages are perfectly in keeping with what we know about immigrant behavior elsewhere. The English in India, in Australia, and even in Canada, are often more conservative in their use of English than the English in Great Britain. Some of them continue to carry on Victorian English formality, such as donning formal wear for dinner parties, while their fellow countrymen at home have undergone revolutionary changes in manners and values and have already accepted the hippies and the Beatles.

Notes

1. Some students claim the differences to be greater between Cantonese and Mandarin as well as among subdialects of Cantonese.

2. Other factors contributing to linguistic unity are the nature of the Chinese written language, discussed in the next section, and the centripetal nature of the Chinese outlook, to be taken up in a later chapter.

3. Joseph Needham (with the collaboration of Wang Ling), *Science and Civilisation in China,* Cambridge University Press. In six volumes: Vol. 1, *Introductory Orientations* (1954); Vol. 2, *History of Scientific Thought* (1956); Vol. 3, *Mathematics and the Sciences of the Earth* (1959); Vol. 4, *Physics and Physical Technology* (Part I, *Physics,* 1962; Part II, *Mechanical Engineering,* 1965; Part III, *Civil and Hydraulic Engineering and Nautical Technology,* in press). The following volumes are in preparation: Vol. 5, *Art of Peace and War* (Part I, *Ammunition, Printing, and Textile*; Part II, *Alchemy and Chemistry*); and Vol. 6, *Biology and Medicine.*

A patriarch and his family. The boy at the extreme right is Bill Way, who appears in another photograph (see insert between pp. 80-81).

Chapter Three

Family and Kinship

When the Honorable P. H. Chang, Chinese Consul-General at New York, was asked by reporters to comment on the low Chinese crime and delinquency rates in the United States, he said:

> Filial piety, the love for parents, is a cardinal virtue my people have brought over from China. . . . A Chinese child, no matter where he lives, is brought up to recognize that he cannot shame his parents. . . . Before a Chinese child makes a move, he stops to think what the reaction of his parents will be.[1]

The Chinese official was speaking of a Chinese cultural characteristic which Westerners have known about for years: the importance of family. But in view of Western prejudice, and to compensate for what they felt to be political, economic, and military inferiority of their own native country, some Chinese have often offered the Chinese way in kinship relationships as a shining example of Chinese superiority. In doing so the Chinese have fallen into an American psychological trap: everything is either all good or all bad, and if it is not all good, it must be bad. This approach is unsound.

The Chinese Family: The Ideal

The Chinese family, according to the traditional ideal, is one in which several generations of married couples live under the same roof. This is the Large

Family ideal in which ancestors on the male side, their spouses, male descendants, and the yet unborn are part of that great whole.

Universally, the human family consists of parents and unmarried children. In some matrilocal and matrilineal societies, the father's role is assumed by the mother's brother, but that is not the case in any of the major societies in the world. Even in that case, the configuration in the basic human cradle is the same as everywhere else: two older persons—one male and one female—and several immature youngsters of either sex.

What differentiates one type of human family from another is the emphasis which each type gives to particular "dyads" [2] in the configuration. In the nuclear family of parents and unmarried children, we can distinguish eight basic dyads: father–son, mother–son, husband–wife, father–daughter, mother–daughter, brother–brother, sister–sister, and brother–sister. Each of these dyads has intrinsic characteristics of its own, called attributes. When a particular dyad is dominant in a particular culture, that dyad tends to modify the functioning of other dyads or even eliminate their consideration altogether. In that case, the attributes of the dominant dyad will overshadow those of other dyads.

A detailed exposition of this view of kinship relationships is found elsewhere.[3] For our present purposes, the reader will be able to appreciate something of this view if he will give himself a simple test.

Suppose your wife and your mother do not get along and your wife comes to you for support. You have basically two alternatives: either you side with her or you side with your mother. Living as you do, in a society where the husband–wife dyad is the dominant one, you must choose to support your wife. You certainly cannot afford to side with your mother; if you do, you cannot make such a view publicly known. If you and your wife happen to live next door to your mother, and if you consult a family counselor, you will be advised to find another house some distance away. Under the circumstances, you cannot even be neutral in the quarrel, for neutrality will be seen by your wife as lack of love and loyalty, in which case she will have the sympathy of relatives and friends alike.

On the other hand, the man in traditional China had to act and think in a totally different direction. Instead of two alternatives he had three: side with his wife, side with his mother, or more or less keep to a neutral course. It was most honorable to side with his mother; all the books told him to do so, and if his wife gave him trouble because of it she would have been judged wrong by all who heard about it. In fact, according to traditional Chinese custom and law, he would have been justified in divorcing her, for a man's relationship with his parents was primary whereas that with his wife was subordinate to it. His marriage, in the first place, brought a daughter-in-law to his parents. "One can always take another wife, but one cannot get another set of parents," so ran a Chinese proverb repeated often in folklore and stories.

I also stated that a traditional Chinese had a third alternative under the circumstances, namely neutrality. This alternative was not the most honorable, and was possible only if the quarrel between his wife and mother were covert.

In that case the man could simply say that he was too busy with livelihood activities to trouble himself with women's affairs or domestic details. But if the tension broke into the open, or if the tension were between his wife and his father, he would have no such freedom of action at all. I must apologize to my modern-day female readers for discussing the situation from the male point of view. The Chinese way of life was male-centered. However, it was a way of life with which the Chinese female had come to terms, and therefore its rules were equally applicable to females. The wife's duties and socially acceptable attitude toward her husband's parents were the same as her husband's. If he quarreled with his father or mother, she had no public alternative except to take the elder's side. The care of a married woman's own parents was the duty of her brothers and their spouses.

Of course, not all Chinese women liked this arrangement, nor do all Americans sent to Vietnam like the war or wish to fight so far away from home. Characteristically, Americans opposed to the Vietnam War have expressed their views loudly, while Chinese women who are dissatisfied with their position and role were not heard from before contact with the West.

With this basic contrast in mind we are in a better position to state the characteristic features of the Chinese family ideal. If the parent–son relationship is primary and permanent, arranged marriage is a logical correlate and marriage by romance is unacceptable. Since romance is based on the sexual attraction between a man and a woman, it tends to be sudden and capricious. That is why we say love is blind. It means the subordination of practical considerations to mutual attraction between two individuals.

But the two Chinese individuals have to live with his parents, his siblings, and his brothers' spouses. With these individuals, it is not romantic attraction that counts but duties, obligations, and the willingness and ability to fulfill them. Consequently, it is never enough for a wife to please only her husband. Her selection has to be determined by how well she will be able to serve her parents-in-law and continue the family line by producing sons. Since the future is always risky and usually beyond man's control, the consultation of horoscopes is often another logical and additional safeguard.

A second feature of the ideal Chinese family is the duty on the part of the sons to support their parents, not in an institution but under the same roof. There is no legal age at which sons and daughters become independent. That is why parental arrangements of marriage are so important. Providing parents with attentive daughters-in-law is part of that support. In fact, the best sons are those who can support their parents in a style better than the one to which they have been accustomed.

But support is only a physical matter. "Dogs and horses can also support their parents," said Confucius.[4] "What is there to differentiate human beings from such beasts if you do not respect your parents?" So, the third feature of the ideal Chinese family is obedience to parental authority and, by extension, to the authority of male ancestors and their spouses. Parental arrangement of marriage is one aspect of it. But this obedience means many additional things. Not violating parental wishes is the obvious one. Not travelling to faraway places during the parents' lifetime is another; if one is compelled by circumstances to travel, he must let his parents know his whereabouts and the time of his return. Not doing anything to defame the parents is a third; in fact, doing everything possible to make them proud is the preoccupation of the filial son. Finally, a good man must not knowingly invite physical danger which may deprive his parents of a son.

However, support and respect of parents is not a one-way street. Parents are intimately and permanently tied to children as are children to parents. Parents are responsible for their sons' education, marriage, and support if the sons are not capable of obtaining these for themselves. Parental duty to daughters is limited to education and marriage. Traditional Chinese custom and law stated that parents had no freedom to dispose of their property as they wished; it belonged to the sons according to the principle of equal division.

Finally, support and reverence toward parents does not stop with the parents' demise. Their spirits must be placed in household and clan shrines, and their remains must be cared for in clan cemeteries. Regular, recurrent rites at the shrines and the cemeteries are the means by which this respect and continued support are shown. Since the spirits of the dead do not enjoy food and other worldly goods in material terms, the Chinese also symbolize their respect and support by burning make-believe money, houses, chests, boats, and cars at funerals and during cemetery visits.

The Chinese Family: The Reality

Reality never completely corresponds to the ideal anywhere; that is the nature of the ideal. But the ideal may be closer to reality in one situation than in another. Insofar as an ideal is consciously upheld by a people, it is bound to have some bearing on reality. The ideal of the Chinese family has a great deal to do with the reality of the Chinese family.[5]

The giant household, consisting of nearly a hundred members and servants, pictured in celebrated novels such as *The Dream of the Red Chamber,* was never a common Chinese occurrence, any more than Captain Ahab of *Moby Dick* fame is to be found among average Westerners. But in each case, the condition of one or a few unusual individuals says something about the majority and provides them with inspirations or models for action. Thus, Chinese literature through the ages was full of exhortations and illustrious examples of how children should please their parents, as well as the ethical rationalization for such behavior. But even the latest unromantic computer-mating schemes in the United States still fail to include parental wishes as a relevant consideration for marriage.

Surveys prior to 1949 show that the average Chinese family consisted of 5.3 members. This was larger than the pre-World War II American average of 3.3, but it was nowhere near the Large Family ideal. What happened was that, among the poor and the modest in means, the husband was more dependent upon his wife for the essentials of life and was thereby forced, under the circumstances, to give greater play to the husband–wife dyad at the expense of the father–son dyad. In that event, the parental household tended to break up as soon as more than one son was married. Since there were many poor families, the average size was bound to be much smaller than the ideal.

But this was only part of the story. The observable fact was that as soon as a family became somewhat better off, it tended to develop in the other direction, toward the Large Family ideal. When that happened, the family would proceed to add all the other trimmings of that ideal to the best of its financial capabilities.

Even the poor household, forced to keep its size small, did not wait until it was better off to make use of the ideal. It had just as much right as the affluent to bury its dead in the clan cemetery and to place the spirit tablets of its dead in the clan temple. The common cemetery and temple were paid for mostly by the well-to-do segments of the clan because that was among the acts a family of high status could use to maintain and increase its status, according to the Chinese ideal. Add to this the universal belief in parental arrangement in marriage, the generalized stigma against flagrant signs of unfilialness, and the long-accepted custom that parents and sons were responsible for each other; it was not surprising that the behavior of the poor and the rich was not basically different. The poor had less opportunity to live up to the socially desirable behavior model, but they did not entertain other notions which deviated to any great extent from the respected ideal.

Wider Kinship

For the Chinese in China, kinship means a tie based first on birth and second on marriage. In fact, the latter is a means to the former. That is why a childless marriage is not much of a marriage. Adoption is therefore to be resorted to reluctantly and the best choice for adoption is the son of a brother, not of a stranger.

Following this logic, we can easily see that relatives outside the parents–children configuration have much more significance for the Chinese than for Americans. Within the large group of related persons, the Chinese differentiate between those born and married to the male line and all others. The first are called *pen chia* (members of the family line); the second are called *ch'in ch'i* (relatives). Women, by virtue of marriage and children, are incorporated into their husband's family lines and assume his surnames.

All *pen chia* share a common surname such as Hsu, Li, Chang, Wong, and so forth. Throughout China the male's attachment to his surname is extremely strong. Consequently the total number of Chinese surnames is very small in proportion to the size of the population. At the core are about 400 to 500 surnames. To this we might add a hundred or so sinicized surnames among Manchus, Mongols, European Moslems, and other tribal individuals, but we still have a very small number. On the other hand, because of civil war, invasion, famine, and the subsequent migrations from one region to another, there are Lis and Changs in different regions of China who claim no kinship with each other, though clans with well-to-do and energetic members were always making efforts to establish genealogical links with lost groups of the same surname.

To further solidify kinship relationships, each financially able clan not only built a clan temple, in which the souls of all the dead would be honored, and developed a clan graveyard, in which the bodies of all the dead would be buried, but it also tended to prearrange naming categories even for the as yet unborn. For the last 15 centuries, nearly all Chinese males have borne a three-character name. The first character is the surname, according to Chinese custom; it also comes first among Japanese, Koreans, Vietnamese, and Hungarians. One of the next two characters signifies the man's generation in the clan and the remaining character is his very own.

Thus, my full name in Chinese is Hsu Lang Kwang; my father's full name was Hsu Chi Shih; and one of my brother's sons (I have no son) was named Hsu T'ien Ch'ung. Hsu is our surname. The characters Kwang, Chi, and T'ien are our names denoting our respective generations. That is to say, my father, all of his brothers, his father's brothers' sons, his father's fathers' brothers' sons' sons, and ad infinitum, bore the name Chi. My brothers, my father's brothers' sons ad infinitum, and I all bear the name Kwang. The same is true of all of my brothers' sons and all of their patrilateral cousins.

In this way, any member of the Hsu clan would know how to address us individually, and any outsider would be able to arrive at a preliminary idea concerning our respective places in our clan organization as soon as he was told our names.[6]

In order to insure the continuation of the rule and to prepare for the as yet unborn, it was not uncommon for a clan to have ten or more names ready in anticipation of their use for as many generations to come. Some generations later, when some of the prearranged characters had been used up by those already born, it would be the duty of some new descendant in the clan to arrange another set of characters for the future. In this way each clan planned for its own continuity and assured itself of an important mechanism to link its past with its future.

Two other things should be noted. When a man travels to another location for any purpose whatever, it is both his obligation and to his advantage to seek out his kinsmen or relatives to join them in whatever they are doing at the time or to assure himself of their help if he needs it. If he made the visit and did not let them know, or if he needed help and availed himself of the assistance of others, he would run the risk of hurt feelings on the part of his relatives and kinsmen in that area. On the other hand, if he sought them out and were refused assistance, he would also have been justified in resenting their nonkinsman- and nonrelative-like behavior.

The other point is that in the absence of true kinsmen or relatives, a Chinese away from home is not averse to relating to his colleagues, employers, and friends in pseudo-kinship terms. Usually this usage is informal. A man normally addresses those much older than he as uncle and aunt, and those of the same age or older as older brother and sister-in-law. By custom he also addresses his friend's grandfather or grandmother in grandfatherly or grandmotherly terms. But often the relationship is formalized, in which case a much older man becomes his "dry father" or he becomes a "sworn brother" of one or more of his friends, colleagues, or employers.

The Chinese custom of sworn brotherhood is not unlike the custom of blood brotherhood reported in many parts of the world. Several men of more or less similar age become related after a ritual before certain gods. Among ancient warriors and members of secret societies the ritual included the physical mixing of blood from a cut in the arm. Among scholars and others the blood exchange is omitted but the other essentials are the same: pooling birth data, obeisance before gods in a temple or in a temporary altar set up for the occasion, firecrackers, and a feast together with or without invited guests. The most favored gods for this purpose were three heroes depicted in the celebrated novel, *The Romance of Three Kingdoms,* based on events at the end of the Han dynasty (206 B.C. to A.D. 220). The three heroes, commonly known by their surnames as Liu, Kuan, and Chang, began their campaigns together by entering into sworn brotherhood. They remained loyal to each other to the end of their days.

A "dry father" is the equivalent of a godparent in the West except that he has nothing to do with religious affiliation. A Chinese may choose to become someone's "dry son" when he is an adult. Or he may do so because his father and a friend decided to strengthen their friendship by an additional bond. In the latter instance a boy becomes the "dry son" of his father's friend. In any case, a "dry son" and his "dry father" also have more ceremonial obligations to each other than a godson to his godfather.

But the bond does not stop there. An American has a godfather; that bond is confined to him and to the older man alone. The latter's wife is his godfather's wife and his children are his godfather's children. Not so with the Chinese. My "dry father's" wife is my "dry mother" and his children are my "dry siblings." Exactly the same thing holds true with reference to sworn brothers' parents, spouses, and children.

Thus, three of the outstanding characteristics of the Chinese way in kinship are also found in its extension: (1) the subordination of the individual to his place in the kinship framework, including its authority; (2) the continuation of the kinship bond through life, regardless of age; and (3) a tendency for the kinship web to spread, once a basis for kinship is established. Of course, the web of kinship is not uniformly intense everywhere. One has many more duties, obligations, and privileges with reference to one's parents than with reference to brothers, more with reference to brothers than with cousins, and so forth. The Chinese have many specific rules governing such gradations. But a Chinese is never free from this web of kinship; as he goes through life, he is likely to have enlarged it.

The Question of Freedom

The reader may wonder how the average Chinese could have tolerated such a lack of freedom over so many centuries. Don't the Chinese want to come out from under the parental yoke? Don't the Chinese want to select their own mates? Don't the Chinese women want to have homes of their own and not live under the "tyranny" of their mothers-in-law?

If we look into the historical record we do find some Chinese instances of unhappiness and tragedy due to kinship restraints. One celebrated case involved a poet who had to divorce his beloved and devoted wife because his mother hated her. Years later when he and she were each married to someone else they chanced upon one another in a public outing. They realized that they were still in love, but all he could do was send her a poem to which she responded with another poem. The poems have stood the test of time. In another case, a learned man, while a guest in someone's house, was playing the lute one night. A newly widowed beauty of his host's house was so enraptured by his music that she eloped with him. There are also stories about sons who ran away from home and high-born girls who married lower-class boys in spite of parental objection.

But these instances did not negate the fact that the Chinese way in kinship gave the individual a great sense of security and the wherewithal to deal with the problems he faced in the world. Women who were not beautiful did not need to frequent lonely hearts clubs. Their marital destinies were assured by their parents. Men who just hoped to get through life with minimum effort did not have to seek their own identity and make a world of their own. If their parents were not poor, all they had to do was to take advantage of the shadow of their ancestors.

One characteristic of the human way of life everywhere is that no individual can live alone. He must have other human beings for whom he cares and who care for him. Mark Twain said something to the effect that "The more I look at human beings, the more I like dogs" only because he was disillusioned and bitter. In turn, his saying easily recalls George Eliot's story of the lonely Silas Marner, whose only preoccupation every evening was to count and polish his coins. When his treasure was stolen and the young girl turned up at his door, Silas Marner had little trouble switching his devotion from the money to the winsome lass.

Consequently, we see human beings everywhere in assemblages; we see them as members of societies and, within each society, we see them banded together with other members into fraternities, moieties, age groups, age grades, neighborhoods, honor societies, elites, aristocracies, literati, clubs or associations, gangs, cliques, orders, and so forth. The most important grouping in Chinese society happens to be the family and its extension, the larger web of kinship. The Chinese has been taught since childhood to seek harmony in that group. It was the human beings in that particular type of group who satisfied the Chinese individual's need for succor, comfort, affection, sympathy, help, exhilaration, and approbation. Why, then, should the Chinese look outside of it? [7]

Notes

1. Quoted in Ed Ritter, Helen Ritter, and Stanley Spector, *Our Oriental Americans* (New York: McGraw-Hill Book Co., 1965), p. 39.

2. A dyad is any relationship formed by two persons, as distinguished from a triad which is formed by three persons.

3. Francis L. K. Hsu, *Kinship and Culture* (Chicago: Aldine Publishing Co., 1971).

4. Confucius obviously did not know much about animals.

5. We cannot, therefore, agree with students of Chinese society who claim, in typically Western all-or-none fashion, that ideals and realities are separate. See Maurice Freedman, Foreword, p. xiii, in Margery Wolf, *The House of Lim* (New York: Appleton-Century-Crofts, 1968).

6. Not all clans or branches of the same clan followed this custom with equal faithfulness. But the custom is well known in China and was certainly common in all parts of China.

7. The facts given in two recent field studies, Margery Wolf's *House of Lim* (New York: Appleton-Century-Crofts, 1968) and Norma Diamond's *K'un Shen* (New York: Holt, Rinehart and Winston, 1969), which deal with the psycho-social aspects of Chinese family structure in Taiwan, support our main contention that Chinese children are trained to value harmony, despite the divisive potentiality of the Chinese kinship group. By contrast, American children are trained to seek self-gratification and be self-centered, a point that will become clear later.

Dr. Francis L. K. Hsu and his family.

Chapter Four

Family Behavior and the American Context

There is no doubt that residence abroad, even for a brief period, creates opportunities for some change in behavior. Respectable English ladies have been known to sow their wild oats in Italy. Many Americans tend to approach waiters and servants in the Orient with a hauteur they would despise at home. I have been told quite a few times by high-caste Hindus that they would not hesitate to eat beef abroad.

When the familiar restraints are absent and new social and cultural ingredients are added, anyone is liable to behave differently. But the extent of change and the kind of change when away from home are not a foregone conclusion. They are very much dependent upon the cultural soil from which the travellers have sprung and the circumstances in which they find themselves abroad.

The examples we have given above are relatively temporary changes. Upon return to their respective homes, we expect the travellers to revert to their original behavior patterns. But people who have left their own society to permanently settle in another are bound to develop more permanent changes. The longer they live in the new environment, the more we must expect them to change. And we must, also, expect the descendants born in the new environment to depart from the ways of their ancestors more than their forebears who came as adult immigrants.

Thus, early American settlers departed from the governmental structure they had known in Europe. They not only dispensed with royalty but did away with most inherited privileges as well. However, it took Americans some time before they abolished primogeniture according to which the eldest son received all of the property and the other sons none. For many years, some Americans were Royalists. Many of them, seeing the writing on the wall, later migrated to Canada and elsewhere. Today one can safely say that no American is a Royalist, although some Americans still favor the English over other Europeans, not to speak of Asians or Africans. The English Speaking Union is still an extremely active social group in many parts of the country.

But the extent and the kinds of permanent changes (a phenomenon known to anthropologists as acculturation) are also not foregone conclusions. They, too, are dependent upon the cultural base from which the immigrants have come and upon the circumstances abroad in which they find themselves.

The Chinese Family in America

It can safely be said that very few Chinese parents in America live with their married sons or daughters.[1] A widow or a widower may do so, which is true also among Whites, but rarely does this occur when both parents are living. This much is certain among the Chinatown-centered Chinese, Hawaii's Chinese, and the Chinese who belong to the scholar and professional group noted in Chapter 1.

Generally speaking, members of the last group are parents and their children from China (whom we shall designate as immigrants hereafter) as well as their first-generation United States–born children (whom we shall designate as United States–born hereafter). This contrasts with the other two groups among whom second- and third-generation United States–born are common. At first glance, we should therefore expect the immigrant scholars and professionals to adhere more to the traditional Chinese family pattern than do their own United States–born children as well as the United States–born children of Hawaiian and Chinatown-centered groups. In reality this is not so for two reasons. The immigrant scholars and professionals were drawn largely from the educated of China's cities and towns. Even in China during the 1930's most of them lived in separate dwellings with or without unmarried children, away from their parents. Many received economic support from their parents if they could not make ends meet, but the idea of forming a so-called "small family" (*hsiao chia t'ing*) was a mark of modernization, and as such both the educated and their parents subscribed to it.

From this point of view, the elimination of the traditional Large Family ideal among all groups of Chinese in America is not solely a result of immigration to the New World. The same Western influence was felt in China itself before Chinese immigrants had settled in the United States. Had the second- and third-generation United States–born Chinese been born in China, and had they also been educated to the same extent, they, too, would have lived apart from their parents.

A second feature of the Chinese family in America is that marriage is no longer parentally arranged. Parents are consulted, and parental consent is still very important, but parents no longer have the entire responsibility. In this, also, the Chinese in America are not different from their educated counterparts in the land of their ancestors. There is a curious contrast here between China on the one hand, and Japan and India on the other—a contrast impossible to explain here. In all three societies, the traditional rule for mate selection was by way of parental arrangement. While the educated in China began as early as the turn of the century to insist on romantic love and freedom of selection, to this day, most educated Japanese and the Hindus have left the matter to their parents.[2]

But there are many more common changes among the Chinese in America than among those in China. One of these concerns intermarriage. Obviously, the Chinese in China do not have the opportunities for intermarriage that the Chinese elsewhere have. Quite a few Chinese students who went abroad did bring non-Chinese wives back with them. The earliest instance of such a marriage occurred in the second quarter of the nineteenth century when Mr. Yung Wing, the first Chinese student to study abroad, received his B.A. from Yale University and married Mary Louise Kellogg from Connecticut. Many Chinese students who studied in Japan married Japanese girls. One of these is Kuo Mo-jo, a well-known literary man who still holds an important position in mainland China today. But such intermarriages were an unusual phenomenon, seldom occurring in large numbers even among returned students.

On the other hand, even quite a few Chinatown-centered Chinese have intermarried with non-Chinese. The rate is higher among scholars and professionals and their children, and highest among Hawaii's Chinese. In 1960 to 1964, 54.8 percent of Chinese marriages in Hawaii involved a non-Chinese bride or groom—half of whom were Japanese, with the other half divided between Caucasians and part-Hawaiians.[3] It is interesting to note that while intermarriage in China as a rule meant Chinese males marrying non-Chinese females, two-fifths of the Chinese–Caucasian marriages and one-third of the Chinese–Japanese marriages in Hawaii involved Chinese brides and non-Chinese grooms.

A third feature of the Chinese family is that the ancestor-worship complex is greatly modified. Ancestral altars at home have nearly disappeared among the Chinese in Hawaii and in mainland United States. I do not know of any Chinese clan cemetery in the United States, although in many American cities white discrimination has led to a number of Chinese cemeteries, where individual families obtain lots in the same way one would purchase lots in all public cemeteries. In 1949 a large number of urns with the ashes of the dead were still waiting to be transported to China from Hawaii for burial in the ancestral cemeteries in or near the deceased's village of origin. This was one of the filial duties of sons whose parents died away from home. The political changes in mainland China since 1949 have made the observance of this custom difficult or impossible. At any rate, by 1970 only a very few such urns can still be found in a minor structure at the Manoa Chinese Cemetery of Honolulu.

In place of traditional Chinese clan organization, in which generation names and lineage affiliations are prominent, along with a clan temple where periodic offerings are made to all past generations of ancestors, the Chinatown-centered and Hawaiian Chinese have among them many family-name associations. A number of these associations are housed in buildings owned by them, and in some of them, a place of honor (resembling an altar) is set up for "All Ancestors of the X Clan." The main function of such associations, however, is social and not ritual.

A new development is for family-name associations in different localities to form a local federation with the head association in San Francisco. The head association will even underwrite part of the local building costs, provided the local counterpart can supply the bulk of the necessary funds; this is very much like the pattern established between the national headquarters of any fraternity or sorority and its local chapters. For example, the Lee Family Association of Honolulu has been encouraged in this way by the San Francisco Lee Family Association, although the Lee Family Association of Honolulu has not yet been able to raise its share of the funds. The San Francisco organization has helped to build club houses for several Lee Family Associations in different parts of the United States.

Tension between the Generations

I do not want to give the impression that intergenerational tensions did not exist in China. Some Chinese novels and dramas featured themes of unfilial sons and their punishments. Many were Chinese tales of troubles between mother-in-law and daughter-in-law. In villages and towns where I was born and grew up, the elders, including my parents, often related to us a probably apocryphal story of a family in which an old man died of an accident because his sons and their spouses had not been dutiful.

This man had three married sons, each of whom owned his own home. By previous agreement, the aged widower was to live in each house for a month at a time. On the day marking the end of one of these months it snowed heavily. The father was supposed to move to another house but he decided that under the circumstances he would wait until the weather was less stormy. The son and his wife, anxious for the old man to leave their home, sent their little boy to remind him that it was time. Thinking it was merely the boy's whimsical remark, the grandfather paid him no heed. But when the little boy came in with the same reminder a second time, the grandfather at once understood its significance. He angrily set out from the house in the snow storm. His body was found the next day under a pile of snow not far away.

This was used as an example for educating children; when family troubles did occur, the unfilial sons and daughters-in-law were objects of public censure. They would certainly be ashamed to admit their actions, much less to brag about them. Given the American environment in which the ideal is for children to be independent of their parents as soon as they can, and where parental authority and kinship ties have negative rather than praiseworthy connotations, we should not be surprised if more Chinese depart from their ancestral ways. In the case of Chinatown-connected Chinese, this situation is often aggravated by the fact that neither the China-born parents' English nor their United States–born children's Chinese is sufficiently fluent for in-depth discussion of their feelings. But tension is by no means rare even without linguistic differences.

In the October 13, 1969, issue of the *Chung Yang Jih Pao (Central Daily News)* published in Taipei, there was a short article entitled, "I Regret Having Sent My Children to America." Although widowed 14 years previously, the writer had worked and succeeded in sending her three daughters and only son to different universities in the United States. Most of them were now married and independent, thus belonging to our scholar and professional group. When the lonely mother wrote from Taiwan to suggest that she visit them, neither of the two older daughters laid out the welcome mat. In fact, the eldest replied that she had better stay home because:

Older people should not come to America. We do not have time to take care of you. It will waste much energy and money. Americans do not live under the same roof with their parents. . . .

The mother nevertheless came and stayed for a while with her only son and his wife. One night she got into a violent argument with the son over what she described as some trivia. In a fit of temper, the young man brought her suitcase to the door and told her to leave. Fortunately, the daughter-in-law saved the day by making her husband apologize to the mother. At the time of the article's writing, the mother was staying with her youngest daughter who consoled her with the following words:

They have been separated from you for so long. That is why they have changed. Please forgive them. After all, they are your own children. One day they will repent. . . .

Obviously, not all Chinese in our scholar and professional group treat their parents with such extreme callousness and lack of sensitivity. In fact, this case came to me as a total surprise, for its counterpart cannot be found in my observations of and experiences with Chinese in America. On the contrary, I have several friends who went to a great deal of trouble to arrange Mah-Jongg partners and other activities or amusements for their non-English-speaking, aged parents.

Shortly after the publication of the article in the Taiwan daily by the disillusioned mother, two sympathetic responses appeared in the same paper.

One was by a 70-year-old Chinese who came from Taiwan about one and a half years ago to be with his children in the United States and had been enjoying himself here. He deplored the disappointed mother's plight but he asked her to understand the preconditions for the change in her children. The correspondent posed a series of questions to her. If she could not drive by herself, did she feel lonesome during the day? Could she speak enough English to converse with guests, to answer the phone, or to amuse herself with television and English publications? If there were grandchildren, could she take care of their diaper and food needs according to the American style? Since her children had to work very hard to keep up with their professional positions (implying that the situation is unlike that of Taiwan or traditional China where, having once arrived, a man can simply take it easy), did she try to relieve the parents of some of their burdens? Or did she simply sit around (like a Chinese mother whose children have made it) and expect them to entertain her? Did one of her children have a chronic stomach ulcer acquired in the process of establishing himself or herself? Could some of these be the preconditions of the violent quarrel with her son "over some trivia"?

The correspondent then reminded the disillusioned mother of the quality of flexibility, which was often asked of the applicants on the many forms required for admission to American universities. He asked: Did not the parents of many applicants declare that their sons and daughters could adapt well because they possessed flexibility? Flexibility means the ability to change; was that not the basic quality which assured her children of their success in America? He ended his article with the plea for a Program of American Studies in Taiwan so that parents who are about to visit their children in America would receive adequate psychological preparation.[4]

The other sympathetic response was from Professor Chang Chen-tung in Taiwan who had spent some six years in America. His article is more analytical of the Chinese–American cultural differences affecting family relationships. Here is a condensation of some of the high points.

Professor Chang offers his sympathy for the disillusioned mother and expresses distaste for her children. But he urges his readers to keep in mind the basic differences between China and the United States. Chinese society is founded on agriculture, in which conservatism, family and filial piety are central. American society is founded on commerce and industry. Chinese ancients long ago noted that merchants love profit at the expense of compassion and justice. Such a society is fluid, especially since its people were immigrants to start with. Although Taiwan has entered the world of commerce and industry, its people still have their inherited family sentiments and human feelings. Therefore, the Chinese students in America have literally jumped into another environment totally alien to them. Those who have had strong training in Chinese ethics will still remember all that their parents did for them, but for those with weaker training in Chinese ethics, it is just too bad.

American society emphasizes independence and emigration. Parents do not have to leave property to their children, so children do not have to support aged parents. There are pensions, Social Security, and annuities to take care of the old. They do not feel any obligation to help their sons and daughters to take care of their grandchildren; consequently, human sentiments suffer by reduction and parents find themselves paying grandparents to baby-sit. These patterns and others are the true expressions of a commercial and industrial society. To a Chinese, such conduct would prove embarrassing, but this is considered natural by most Americans. Thus, because of this cultural divergence, Chinese elders find it much more difficult to accept these actions. The Chinese youth, however, who has not yet been so thoroughly attuned to his own society can adjust more easily to the American way of life.

Adding to such basic differences is the fact that the Chinese from Taiwan do not have an easy time during their studentship. Money is always short and many of them have had to work as waiters, dishwashers, or baby-sitters. The monetary difficulty they experience during that period has easily led them closer to the American "money first" philosophy. For short visits by kinsmen, a host can still be friendly with enthusiasm, but a longer sojourn makes enthusiasm impossible. The latter event is especially likely to be the case if your children's spouses are American-born or non-Chinese.

Concluding the article, Professor Chang surmises that the children of the disillusioned mother probably had very little training in Chinese ethics, for he has seen throughout his six years in America very few cases of such unfilial behavior. He observed that many students who had to wash dishes to make their way through school even remitted part of their wages to parents in Taiwan. Professor Chang hopes that Chinese students going to America would be given more training in Chinese ethics, before leaving home, and that "The Renaissance of Chinese Civilization," currently an official movement in Taiwan, will spread to all corners of the earth.[5]

Some readers will note that Professor Chang probably erred by saying that grandparents are paid for baby-sitting. My observation is that American elders are divided into those who will oblige happily and those who do not want to be bothered. I also have good reason to disagree with his view that a non-Chinese spouse necessarily aggravates the situation. Others will note that Professor Chang is not quite consistent, for if, according to him, the American type of parent–child relationship is a function of a commercially and industrially based society, how can the "Renaissance of Chinese Civilization," which promotes, among other virtues, agriculturally-based filial piety, spread to all corners of the earth?

However, in spite of such minor points, Professor Chang's observations of Chinese–American differences as they affect the behavior of Chinese students and scholars are sound. And the case of the disillusioned mother from Taiwan bears strange similarity to the plight of a United States–born Chinese mother in California. The latter, too, is a widow, except that her children were edu- cated and married before her husband passed away. She has three sons and two daughters and many grandchildren, all of whom went to private schools and first-rate colleges. She is financially quite independent, but her problem is, as she puts it, "My children don't want me anymore."

Some years before her husband died, she became interested in and then a zealot of Jehovah's Witnesses. From the beginning of her widowhood, church work became her life. Like all Jehovah's Witnesses, she rings doorbells and expounds the Truth. Only one son and one daughter live in the same city with her, so she visits them regularly. She has always been a selfless mother and now she acts like a very good Chinese grandmother, taking care of her grandchildren whenever called on to do so, bringing gifts to the son's and daughter's homes for adults and children alike, and teaching the grandchildren Biblical stories from the vast store of Jehovah's Witnesses literature.

One day when she came to her daughter's home for another session with the grandchildren, she was greeted by the young woman with a bundle of Jehovah's Witnesses literature. The daughter had collected all the leaflets and books the widow left for the grandchildren and told her mother that "we do not want the children to learn this anymore." From her son's wife (who happens to be White) the widow received even sterner words to the same effect. Since then, she has only been able to see her grandchildren occasionally, for the daughter and daughter-in-law no longer ask her to baby-sit.

The widow is regretful; if she had to do it over again, she would discourage college education, at least for the girls. Then they would not be so independent and probably would accept the Lord as she does and might be closer to her.

Thus, in different ways, two Chinese widows on opposite sides of the Pacific have the same problem. The problem is not absent in China, considering the fact that the average modern college-educated Chinese must differ from his parents in culture and experience by at least a century. But if the two widows and their children were in Taiwan today, or in mainland China before 1949, the outcome would have been different and, more importantly, not so abrupt. Even today, the children of the widow from Taiwan could not possibly maintain their respectability if they dared behave in such an unfilial and unfeeling way within a purely Chinese context. What if she did not busy herself to help her daughters-in-law and if she did not know the new-fangled ways of taking care of children and babies? Grandmothers are supposed to enjoy themselves, especially if they are fortunate enough to have successful children. Don't Chinese grandparents have power over their grandchildren? That, too, is part of Chinese filial piety and is what Professor Chang alludes to when he speaks of preparing students with stronger training in Chinese ethics before they go abroad.

In a purely Chinese context, the American-born widow would have found other and probably more rewarding activities than those of an eager Jehovah's Witness. For one thing, Chinese friends and relatives do not isolate widows in their midst as do Americans. A widow in America will be flooded with overwhelming attention for the week or so following her husband's funeral. After that she is likely to become a third leg or, if she is attractive, a threat wherever she goes. She may need to resort to proselytization as a way of being close to her grandchildren; but in the Chinese context, even in disagreement, her children would be less abrasive. Furthermore, I have never seen or heard of Chinese widowed grandmothers doing missionary work. However, the

Chinese–American contrasts in religious behavior will be dealt with in a later chapter.

Discontinuity and Exclusiveness

A United States–born mother whose parents came from a subdistrict in Chung Shan tried her best to dissuade her son from marrying a United States–born girl whose parents were of Hakka extraction; the son nevertheless married her. When the daughter-in-law was three months pregnant, the mother-in-law, who lived in another house with her husband and other children, would call the younger woman on the phone frequently and say something like, "I hope your child is stillborn," or "I hope he will be born defective."

A grandfather from Taiwan joined his son and daughter-in-law permanently. The younger couple made him very welcome and showed every consideration as a Chinese son and daughter-in-law should. After six months, their American-born six-year-old son could contain his curiosity no longer. He asked in front of the elder, "Why does Grandpa stay here all the time? Does he have no home of his own?"

I cannot be absolutely certain that no mother-in-law in China would be so venomous toward a son's spouse whom she disliked, or that no grandson in China would ask such an embarrassing question in front of his grandfather. I can, however, say that such attitudes and questions are highly improbable in the Chinese context.[6]

Any mother is likely to find her son's wife more or less threatening by virtue of the fact that the younger woman is taking over her own creation. But a mother-in-law, in the Chinese way of life, is less threatened because the continuity of the generations and inclusiveness of the Big Family ideal provide her with some protection; these same attributes also mean that her daughter-in-law's children are part of her. If they are stillborn or if they are defective, that condition will reflect on her. In Chinese thinking, people may well interpret the misfortune as retribution for some sort of misconduct on the part of the older woman. She cannot be so outwardly venomous toward the younger woman because of sheer self-interest.

Likewise, a six-year-old boy in China would have understood that it is not unnatural for grandparents to be part of the family; he would have seen that to be the case in neighbors' and relatives' homes. Even when grandparents live separately from his parents, the older man and woman do not behave like guests when they come to visit. Furthermore, even if the boy felt like asking the question he would have been socialized enough by Chinese rules to refrain from such an overt expression of his private doubts.

The American cultural context is characterized by resistance to authority, discontinuity between the generations and exclusiveness of the parent-children unit. All are upheld as high values; two are buttressed by law, custom, and sage writings. The Chinese mother-in-law in America suffers from American-type pressures and is therefore liable to American-type defenses. If a Chinese grandson in America has had only the American type of narrow and self-indulgent experiences, he, too, tends to feel free to question circumstances he regards as abnormal.

Notes

1. In Hawaii, I know of two households in which parents live with their married children and unmarried grandchildren. In one case the parents occupy one house and their married daughter, her husband, and their children occupy another house on the same lot. They cook, eat, and share all other activities together. In Chinatowns in San Francisco and other mainland cities, a common pattern is for a family to own an apartment building in which parents occupy one unit and adult married children occupy others. But they usually do not have their daily meals together.

2. For explanation of this contrast see F. L. K. Hsu, *Clan, Caste, and Club* (Princeton, N. J.: D. Van Nostrand and Co., 1963), and F. L. K. Hsu, *Iemoto: The Heart of Japan* (in preparation).

3. Andrew Lind, *Hawaii's People* (Honolulu: University of Hawaii Press, 1967), p. 110.

4. *Chung Yang Jih Pao* (*Central Daily News*), Taipei, Taiwan, December 10, 1969.

5. *Chung Yang Jih Pao* (*Central Daily News*), Taipei, Taiwan, November 11, 1969.

6. Dr. Kenneth A. Abbott, who has devoted much of his scholarly energy to studying the Chinese in the United States and whose wife is a San Francisco–born Chinese, reminds me that the Chung Shan mother-in-law who is so antagonistic to her Hakka daughter-in-law may have been "acting on the basis of her Chinese values." Abbott continues: "Chung Shan people rarely marry Hakka. It is similar to a New England Yankee marrying a Southern Negro. In both cases there *should* be no objections, but feelings run high. The Hakka wars of the nineteenth century indicate that the marriage would have a difficult time." (Personal communication.) I do not entirely subscribe to this view. Northern Chinese and Cantonese rarely intermarried in China, but in the two cases of such intermarriage I did know, each of the mothers-in-law relented after initial opposition. Besides, the leader of the Taiping Rebellion (1850–1864) was a Hakka. He began his campaign in Kwangtung Province and non-Hakka Cantonese followers contributed much to his success.

Annual meeting of a family name association in Hawaii.

Chapter Five

The Attraction
of Local Ties

The Chinese respondents to the disillusioned mother's complaint see the American–Chinese contrasts as founded on the differences between a commerce- and industry-based way of life and an agriculture-based one. This view is not their invention. It is a view that has always been used by American sociologists and historians to explain the "superiority" of or at least the differences between American developments and developments in other countries.

A more sophisticated version of this essentially economic interpretation of history is the Frontier Thesis by the American historian, Frederick J. Turner. In the environment of an undeveloped continent, the pioneers had a need for and found a degree of self-sufficiency which they did not experience in their homelands. The self-sufficiency of those who survived produced, in pioneer Americans and many of the later immigrants, an undeniable ruggedness of character, a degree of mastery over the environment, and a feeling of individual importance which provided the foundation for self-reliance and the flowering of the American way of life. This is the gist of Turner's thesis.[1]

It is difficult to see how the need for self-sufficiency and a vast frontier could have been all that were necessary for the birth of the American way of life. The average Chinese farmer with five or more acres of land could produce practically all he and his family needed: food, clothes, housing, and even transportation. Centuries ago, many Chinese migrated to Manchuria where land was cheap, opportunities abundant, and the conditions of life paralleled those of the early American West in several ways. But the Chinese in

Manchuria never developed an outlook even remotely similar to that of the American because Chinese self-sufficiency was a result of circumstances, not of choice. As soon as a man could leave his farm to live the life of an absentee landlord in some town or city, he not only ceased to be self-sufficient in fact, but he consciously tried to forget the entire experience as well. This was so because the Chinese did not entertain any idea that man *should* be self-sufficient.

The self-sufficiency of pioneer Americans was rooted in fierce individualism which is the mainspring of the American way of life. This frontier-induced self-sufficiency was a channel into which their individualism could flow without restraint. Thus unfettered individualism became an ideal which Americans inculcated into their children and in terms of which they judged the worth of all mankind.

Noah versus Yu

The tradition of each people is likely to be embodied in myths which are enjoyed, dramatized, and transmitted from generation to generation. They are inspirational and are used as justification for present and future behavior. Not infrequently, the same basic mythical theme is embellished and changed by different peoples; each group must have something to suit its own psychological taste. Certainly this is the case with the contrasting Western and Chinese versions of the same mythological primeval flood legend.

The reader is familiar with the Western version. As punishment for the wickedness of men, God decided to flood the earth and kill all except the chosen man, Noah, and his immediate family. Noah made an ark into which he packed his wife, his three sons and their wives, together with pairs of animals to escape the disaster. After some 40 days the flood subsided and the ark landed on Ararat. Upon landing, Noah thanked the Lord by performing the appropriate rituals. Then he and his wife lived together for awhile with their sons. One day Noah drank the wine he had made and, while under the influence of liquor, exposed himself in his tent. Ham saw his father's condition first and told his two brothers about it. Shem covered his father, but there ensued a quarrel after which Noah showed favoritism by blessing Shem and Japheth while cursing Ham and condemning Ham's son Canaan as well as his descendants to be the slaves of Shem and Japheth forever. In the end, the sons and their wives all went their separate ways.

The salient features of the Western version of the myth stand out clearly. Noah and his family members did not return to the place of their origin. In preparation for the disaster, Noah did not do anything about his parents.[2] After the flood, he and his family members did not even make any gesture in that direction, nor did Noah think about his father's or mother's graveyard back home. Furthermore, Noah and his family members did not remain together long; they quarreled and then separated in anger.

It is interesting that in the Babylonian version of the flood, from which the ancient Hebrews derived theirs, King Xisurus built the boat which carried not only family members but also friends. Before the flood, he ordered a complete record to be made of all existing knowledge and buried it. After the flood, King Xisurus went to heaven but his people returned home. One can only interpret the Hebrew revision of the myth as commensurate with their view of man, God, and things. It certainly has set the tone for the husband–wife-centered kinship system of the individualistic Western tradition, of which the American way of life is its most illustrious descendant.

The contrast between the Western version of the myth and its Chinese counterpart is truly startling. The Chinese account begins with two great moral rulers, Emperors Yao and Shun (said to have reigned respectively between 2357–2258 B.C. and 2258–2206 B.C.). In Yao's old age, a terrible flood devastated the country. Yao appointed Kun to control the flood, but Kun was unsuccessful. Yao resigned in self-reproach and renounced the throne to Shun as his successor. Emperor Shun exiled the failure, Kun, and appointed Kun's son, Yu, in his place. Yu worked for 13 years, traveling all over the country, and he succeeded in eradicating the flood. Three different times during his tour of duty he passed his own house where his wife and children lived, but he did not enter it. After his success, Yu was offered the throne by the grateful Emperor Shun.

The Chinese version does not name any chosen man (as Noah was) for God's favor; instead all Chinese were to be saved from the disaster. The Chinese version does not even say only the Chinese (or one group among them) should take refuge in a boat or flee the country; instead it clearly expresses the notion that they must remain where they were born and raised and control the flood as best they could. The Chinese never have evinced a need to seek a utopia where all problems can be solved. The Chinese version offers no possibility for the sons to go in different directions from their fathers; instead Yu worked hard to succeed where Kun failed, thereby not only vindicating his father's name but also giving honor to his ancestors and benefits to his yet unborn descendants. Finally, Yu put his larger duty before matters of his own heart and did not even see his family during the length of his service.

Thus the Chinese version of the flood and its aftermath set the standard of behavior for the father–son-dominated kinship system of China which developed into a lasting tradition of mutual dependence among men as its most important characteristic.

The Chinese tradition, which emphasized the group and conventional authority, staying in the same place, and continuation of the father–son link, was later systematized, sharpened, and made more specific by Confucius and his followers in their concept of a kinship organization anchored in filial piety. The Western counterpart—which glorifies the individual and his spouse, moving away from the homeland in defiance of the group, dispersing into different parts of the world—can be found in Jesus and his followers, who labored to decimate the power of family and kinship. It was Jesus who said,

Brother will deliver up brother to death, and the father his child; and children will rise against parents, and have them put to death.[3]

Lack of Desire to Emigrate

The contrasting versions of the flood myth are not meaningless stories; they have guided Western and Chinese behavior for centuries. A most spectacular proof of this conclusion is found in the actual patterns of Western and Chinese emigration.

The Chinese as a whole have never shown any great propensity for moving away from China. The Chinese simply did not entertain the notion, so prevalent among Western peoples, of finding a new world and separating themselves from the past and from the land of their ancestors. Indeed as we noted in a previous chapter, the Chinese has always tended to return to his homeland even if circumstances compelled him to seek fame and fortune elsewhere. Were he to die abroad, it would be the duty of his sons to return his bones to China for burial. This homeward-looking tendency was, in fact, used by the United States as one factor justifying its anti-Chinese acts.

Now it is perfectly true that today there are sizeable Chinese communities in many Southeast Asian countries. Forty percent of Malaysia's population is Chinese, and about ten percent of the Thai population is Chinese.[4] But when we shift the focus and see the matter in probability terms, we obtain a different picture. Had the Chinese been inclined to emigrate as were the Irish and Swiss, or indeed all Western Europeans, it should not be hard to see the probability that today most of Southeast Asia and many other parts of the world would have been dominated by Chinese instead of Westerners.[5]

The truth is that, in spite of poverty, dynastic changes, and invasions by tribal peoples from the North and the Northwest, very few Chinese—in proportion to the total Chinese population—have ever left China. The Chinese who went to Southeast Asia were overwhelmingly of Fukien and Kwangtung origin. If we count only what is traditionally called China Proper, Fukien and Kwangtung are but two of its eighteen provinces.[6] The Chinatown-centered Chinese and Hawaii's Chinese, who make up the bulk of Chinese in the United States today, are emigrants or their descendants from one of the same two provinces, Kwangtung. Only a small number of Chinese from Shantung and Chekiang, two other maritime provinces, emigrated to Japan and Korea over the centuries.

Furthermore, the ancestors of the Chinese in the South Seas and the United States did not even come from the whole of Fukien and Kwangtung. For example, 90 percent of the Chinese in Hawaii originated from one district in Kwangtung province—Chung Shan (formerly Hsiang Shan), the birthplace of Dr. Sun Yat-sen. About 80 percent of the forebears of the Chinese in mainland United States were from Ssu Yi (See Yap, or four districts) next to Chung Shan.

The natives of the South Manchurian village where I was born—in spite of the fact that their ancestors came from Shantung province because of famine—had no emigrant psychology or tradition. The same was true of the people of West Town in Southwestern China where I did part of my field work.[7] Even though many of their ancestors came from Eastern China, a fact they note in their treasured genealogical books, the Yunnanese, too, were void of that psychology or tradition. Throughout my travels and sojourns in North and Central China I found nothing to contradict this picture. They simply did not see emigration as one of the solutions to their problems.

This fits in well with Chinese behavior following the military conquests of their rulers. The Chinese people did not emigrate nor did they insist that others adopt their way of life. If some non-Chinese peoples were voluntarily attracted to the Chinese way of life and wished to become Chinese, they were not prevented from doing so. Thus, quite a few Vietnamese and even some Caucasian Jews, learned in the Confucian classics, successfully took the Chinese Imperial Examinations and became officials of considerable rank. But the Chinese people never went out as missionaries, and Chinese rulers never sent armies to foreign lands to spread Confucianism or the Chinese way of ancestor worship. All the missionaries of the world were and are European or American, not Chinese.[8]

Even in the T'ang dynasty (618–907 A.D.), when some 3,000 devout Chinese monks went separately over a period of many decades to India in search of the true teachings of Buddha, *it was for the purpose of bringing them back to China and not to impose Chinese religion and philosophy on India.*

Chinese Organization in America

This inward-looking tendency of the Chinese was, as we saw before, correlated with a strong family and kinship bond. The link was a two-way street: the initial tendency found expression in the strengthening and elaboration of that bond, and the resulting web of kinship further nurtured and escalated that inward-looking tendency.

The Family Name Association

When the Chinese went abroad and left most of their kinsmen at home, one of their first thoughts was to group themselves along pseudo-kinship lines. Thus we have, in Chinatowns throughout the United States mainland and in Hawaii, many family name associations. New York's Chinatown has about 60 such associations; Hawaii possesses a similar number. These are organizations bearing such names as Moy, Gee, Yee, and so forth. It is difficult to give a precise number either of the associations or of the members in each, for they have a fluidity which will become clear below.

There are two observable tendencies. On the one hand, individuals bearing the same surname may belong to two or more family name associations. For example, there are two Lee Family Associations in New York City, and there are three family name organizations in San Francisco either wholly or in part composed of Chinese bearing the family name of Tan (Tom or Thom).[9] This is because they did not all come from the same locality in Kwangtung and a common genealogical kinship between the separate groups of Lees and Tans had not been established before. In addition, the same family association is subdivided into smaller organizations on the basis of lineage. The Chans in New York, for example, have about 20 such lineage organizations.

In contrast to this tendency to divide from within, people bearing one family name band together with those bearing certain others to form one family association. The "Four Brothers" Association of New York and San Francisco, and the Lung Kang Chung Ch'in Hui of Hawaii consist of Chinese with four names: Liu, Kuan, Chang, and Chao. Part of the reason is that separately they do not have a sufficient number of people for organizing purposes. The rationale for the alliance of these particular four names is rooted in a historical incident depicted in *The Romance of Three Kingdoms* already mentioned in Chapter 3, but with a slight modification. According to that novel, only the three heroes—Liu, Kuan, and Chang—entered into a sworn brotherhood; the hero, Chang, was merely one of the dashing generals serving the senior of the sworn brothers, Liu. In other instances, the pseudo-kinship bond is most contrived. The bearers of the names Tam, Tan, Hsu, and Hsieh in New York, San Francisco, and Hawaii are banded together into one association because the four words have the same radical (component) in common. Those bearing the names Chin, Hu, and Yuan form one association in San Francisco, Sacramento, Los Angeles, New York, Boston, and elsewhere. They claim to be the descendants of the mythological Emperor Shun of great antiquity.

The Locality Associations

In addition to family name associations, the Chinatown-centered and Hawaiian Chinese resort to another type of organization which existed in China for centuries and is not incommensurate with the inward-looking tendency of the Chinese. This is the locality organization generally called *t'ung hsiang hui* (same village association), or *hui kuan* (society or club). The two terms are used interchangeably, except that the latter is usually applied when the organization has a building of its own.

T'ung hsiang hui, or *hui kuan,* is an age-old Chinese organization away from home. The reader will gain a better idea if he will try to visualize these in terms of an organization of Chicago traders in New York called Chicago Hui Kuan or of North Dakota and South Dakota office-seekers and office-holders in Washington, D.C., called Two-Dakotas Hui Kuan.

Thus, the natives of nearly all provinces of China had a *hui kuan* in Peking, the national capital. A not-so-prosperous province might have a joint *hui kuan* with another province to save expenses. These were financed by natives of the respective provinces and each provided hostelry, contacts, and general assistance to its native travellers to Peking for any purpose whatsoever. The inhabitants of a prosperous and commercial city might also establish a *hui kuan* for the benefit of the travellers from that city alone. Finally there were also *hui kuan* in provincial capitals and metropolitan centers such as Hankow and Shanghai.

This is the model for Chinese locality organizations in the United States, and it, too, has exhibited the same tendencies previously noted for the family name associations. On the one hand, many locality organizations are each a combination of Chinese from several districts. Only one of the famous *Chinese Six Companies* of San Francisco,[10] for example, was composed of people from a single district (in this case T'ai Shan, or Toy Shan in Cantonese), while the members of all the others were extractions from two or more districts. In fact, a coordinating organization of all these district associations came into being about 1850 with the name of Chung Hua Hui Kuan (Chinese Society). In 1901, this organization was incorporated under the laws of the State of California as the Chinese Consolidated Benevolent Association.

On the other hand, distinctions based on local units smaller than the district have continued to draw members of the district organizations into separate though nonexclusive groupings. In Hawaii there is a Chung Shan T'ung Hsiang Hui for people from Chung Shan district. But there are also separate subdistrict associations made up of people from eight subdistricts of Chung Shan district such as Liang Tu (Leong Doo), Sze Ta Tu (See Dai Doo), Lung Tu (Lung Doo), and so forth; and there are many village associations each made up of people from a specific village belonging to each of the subdistricts. Thus, Pei T'ai (Pak Toy) T'ung Hsiang Hui is open to all persons of Pei T'ai origin—Pei T'ai being only one of eighteen villages of the subdistrict Liang Tu, in the district Chung Shan.

The association of Hakkas, called Jen Wo Hui Kuan Association (association of human harmony) in San Francisco and Ch'ung Cheng Hui Kuan (following the right way association) in Honolulu, is partly based on locality and partly on dialect. It consists of Hakka-speaking members whose ancestors lived in several districts in Southern Kwangtung province, especially the Mei (Moy) district. The reader will recall that Hakka is one of the seven dialects strongly divergent from all other Chinese dialects and Mandarin.

The Organizational Characteristics

It is not my purpose in this book to list all Chinese organizations old and new. Instead, I propose to examine Chinese patterns of behavior in contrast to their American counterparts and to show how those patterns have fared among the Chinese in America. From this point of view, certain definite Chinese organizational characteristics become clear.

The first is that the idea of kinship solidarity is still important among the Chinese in America, for alleged kinship and pseudo-kinship are obviously prevalent bases for many of their organizations.

Next to kinship, their main emphasis is locality. If men have been trained to see their kinship ties as precious, they are likely to value their local ties as well. When kinship ties are not readily available, local ties are the next logical substitute.

Accordingly, the next two things to be observed are the absence of any cause-promoting orientation and a reluctance to work toward expanded organizational wholes. Kinship and locality emphases are both extremely concrete links among men; recruitment criteria are highly specific and limited. Cause-promoting (for example, temperance or the belief in a particular God) and greatly expanded organizational wholes are much more abstract propositions. At any rate, they involve venturing into untrodden paths. The Chinese in China have not shown a propensity for these activities over the centuries; the Chinese in America have not diverged from this pattern.

The latter observation finds its best substantiation in an examination of (1) how Chinese organizations in America have developed their objectives and carried them out over the years and (2) the newer organizations to which the Chinese have devoted themselves since the days of the tong wars.

For example, many American organizations have suffered from internal divisions as a result of irreconcilable views. But the history of Chinese organizations is characterized by fissions according to family name or locality affiliations.[11] However, the associational affiliations, whether or not they are rooted in fission, are never absolute. For example, individuals bearing the name Chen (Chin) belong simultaneously to (1) the association combining three surnames, (2) that composed exclusively of Chens, and (3) that organized by Chens of a particular locality. This nonexclusive pattern of affiliation is widespread, exactly like the Chinese way in religion, to be discussed in the next chapter.

The aims and activities of these organizations within the last 100 years have differed little from the past, although some of their former functions have been taken over by other newer organizations. For example, the Chinese Chambers of Commerce and Chinese Junior Chambers of Commerce now serve as a commercial clearing house in handling business transactions among the Chinatown-centered Chinese. The Chinese–American Citizens Alliance in San Francisco, the Mid-West Chinese American Civic Association, and other like organizations now deal with legal problems. For many years, the shipment of bones or ashes of dead Chinese back to China was the duty of the district associations. (Such shipment has not been possible since the political change in 1949. It is doubtful that many descendants will resume that Chinese custom even if it were to become possible in the future.)

In the meantime, the desire to link the ancestry of a particular family name association with some illustrious person, real or legendary, remains strong. We noted previously how several family name associations used historical or mythological figures or happenings as the basis for combining several family names in one association. This usage is ubiquitous even for associations in which all members bear the same surname. Thus the Liang (Leong) Family Association honors Liang T'an-Kung as its "first ancestor." The latter was one of the seventy-two high disciples of Confucius. The Lee Family Association honors Lee Er as its "first ancestor." This legendary figure was allegedly the founder of Taoism and the author of the Taoist scripture *Tao Te Ching*. All family name associations have their own "first ancestor" from Chinese history or mythology, and his birthday (real or imagined) is a major festive occasion for the members of the association. In addition, the premises of the association often have a sort of hall of ancestors for worship of the actual ancestors of the members. The only modification from a traditional clan temple in China is that only the tablets of those ancestors will be included whose living descendants have made financial contributions to the association. By this means, the tablets of yet living ancestors may be installed in the hall.

With the reduction in traditional responsibility because of these and other reasons (for example, Chinese in America make increased use of non-Chinese public agencies), a few old Chinese organizations have taken on new purposes and functions. A number of family associations in San Francisco and elsewhere provide low-cost meals for the elderly poor, meet the new immigrants, and more rarely, feature credit unions. But these are not significant departures from the past. Many associations feature a "Women's Division," and a "Youth Division," but these are usually no more than plaques on separate office doors for window dressing. Some of them provide small scholarships for deserving children among their members. Each organization generally has an annual picnic and an annual banquet for members and some guests. The highlight of the latter event consists of the meal itself (usually a very good nine-course Chinese dinner), stereotyped speeches by some Chinese consular official and heads of other organizations, installation of numerous new officers, and the introduction of illustrious guests. One does not have a chance to socialize to any appreciable extent, as each member or guest is seated by prearrangement at a round table for ten in the crowded hall of a restaurant. There is no mixer before or after the dinner; people eat and leave.

There is little in the activities of these organizations that would interest the younger generation in spite of the introduction of some youth activities. The scholarship awards mentioned before are usually so small that they are no more than pocket money for their recipients. At the annual banquets and picnics there are many pre-teen children and babes in arms in accordance with the usual Chinese custom of mixing the generations. Even when a few teenagers are present, they are no more than silent participants. On the other hand, I know one locality assocation (Sze Ta Tu Hui Kuan) in Honolulu which used to invite its young to make use of its four-story club house. However, after some dances and other events, the elders complained that the place had been abused, and the invitation was withdrawn.

Some Chinese organizations, notably the Chinese Chambers of Commerce and the United Chinese Benevolent Societies variously located in Hawaii, Chicago, San Francisco, New York, and elsewhere, have staged Chinese beauty contests for a good many years. These are literally so artificially grafted on to the Chinese cultural body that they have so far produced no cohesive bond between the young and the old. The Chinese generations are tied together in the kinship arena. They have as yet shown no significant tendency to gravitate outside of it, so that the kinship base would become less important or be replaced.

Even the once militant and disreputable tongs (at one point there were at least fifty of them in San Francisco alone) have either disappeared or kept apathetic silence. Only about five of them survive to this day, each with a considerable amount of property, but each almost totally inactive. One cannot help but note the drastic difference between the Italian Mafia and the Chinese tongs. Although they are similar in their gangster behavior, characterized by illegal dealings and violence, the Chinese illegal activities of the tongs rose and ended in less than fifty years as the Chinese in America became among the most law-abiding of all citizens. In contrast, the Mafia's hold on crime, politicians, and the police has become more flagrant over the years.

Why has tong activity disappeared? In view of our analysis the answer is fairly simple but its comprehension requires revision of some usual assumptions. We think of crusaders as promoting socially desirable causes, but they can also promote socially deleterious causes or even totally antisocial causes without any redeeming feature. Being close to their kinship and local bases, the Chinese have never promoted causes on a large scale or attempted to make the world over according to their private design. No Chinese counterparts of Night Riders or Ku Klux Klan have ever developed in China for the purpose of saving China for the Han Chinese alone. The Chinese in America have not actively participated in crusades to save animals or souls.

The Chinese gangsters in San Francisco knew a good thing when they saw it. White prejudice, the ignorance and timidity of most Chinese at the time, and the bribable American police and other officials all combined to make a field day for them, and they flourished. But once circumstances change, people who have no zeal to be missionaries or crusaders—even those with criminal or nonconformist tendencies—are much more likely to mind the writing on the wall and abandon a lost cause. Crusaders and missionaries must have single-minded commitments to specific causes no matter how far they have strayed from the accepted boundaries of respectability of the society as a whole.[12] Even the Chinese in America have not departed that far from the ways of their ancestors.[13]

The newer organizations which the Chinese in America have developed are therefore either extensions of the traditional ones or reactions to or imitations of those of the White majority. Thus in San Francisco the newer Chinese Golf Club and Engineers Club are not run in the traditional Chinese pattern. The same is true of Chinese Lions and Square and Circle which contributed much to social welfare and to the war effort during World War II.[14]

Some twenty-five years ago an American–Chinese Club came into existence in Hawaii. Since the *haoles* (Whites) had their exclusive Pacific Club, Oahu Country Club, and Elks, why shouldn't the Chinese follow suit? It occupied a good piece of real estate on the banks of the Ala Wai Canal, featured spacious, elegantly furnished recreation and conference rooms, and organized banquets, dances, and other social activities. The club's charter members numbered some two hundred, each of whom put up $1,000 to make the venture possible. Soon the membership became less exclusive and non-Chinese were admitted. Then some members saw a business opportunity in the sharply rising real estate prices, and a small group persuaded the other investors in the club to sell their shares for $3,000. It was a tidy profit for a man who less than ten years ago had put in $1,000. The small group of entrepreneurs who bought all the shares then ceased to operate the club and sold the property to developers for a price many times higher than that paid to charter members.

In discussing the vicissitudes of the club, a Chinese banker who was a charter member commented, "We got our money back." A Chinese dentist, also a charter member, held a different view: "I told them they should not have sold the property at the time. It would have been worth many more millions a little later!" The issue of an exclusive club as an answer to White exclusiveness was entirely forgotten.

The Chinese in Hawaii also have a Mandarin Speakers' Club consisting of those who speak Mandarin, who are therefore mostly non-Cantonese. Its membership is, on the whole, drawn from the scholars and professionals group, but here again, no precise criteria for admission are used. In fact, the Mandarin speech of some of the members is not quite intelligible. Its program is not different from that of the Hakka speakers' association, locality associations, or family name associations. The Chinese in mainland United States and in Hawaii also have fraternities and sororities. One of these has the name of Rho Psi, two Greek letters in the fashion of American fraternities, and the Chinese name of Su Yu She (society for respecting friends). Another bears the English letters F.F. and the Chinese name, Chi Lan She (society for a collection of orchids). Rho Psi was founded by Chinese who received a good deal of abuse in the hands of Greek letter fraternities. It began in 1916 at Cornell University and now has eleven chapters, ten in America and one in Hongkong; its headquarters are now located in the Drexel Institute of Technology of Philadelphia. At its last convention in a San Francisco hotel with an attendance of about 120, a joint banquet and ball with two other Chinese fraternities was attended by some 500 revelers.

The most impressive Chinese convention I have attended was that of the Chinese Engineers and Scientists Association of Southern California in 1971. It began with the presentation of technical papers concerned with "New Trends in Engineering and Sciences." It concluded with a banquet in the Grand Ballroom of the Sheraton–Universal Hotel attended by nearly 400 persons, with speeches, awards, entertainment, dancing, and a film presented by a vice-president of North American Rockwell Company showing the highlights of the Apollo 14 successes. It was a glittering event; its content and style were totally dissimilar to those of any Chinatown-connected event, and almost identical with hundreds of American professional conventions except for the lack of excessive drinking (to the hotel bartenders' chagrin), and the sedate manner of the dancing (I did not see one couple holding each other cheek to cheek).

As the generations move on, the Chinese in the United States will undoubtedly develop more organizations based on ties other than kinship and local origin. But three observations are in order. First, the Chinese kinship and locality organizations will persist for a long time to come. Second, in spite of finding little attraction in such organizations, the newer generations of United States–born Chinese will be slow in initiating or joining cause-oriented activities, especially if the causes are of an abstract nature. Finally, as time goes on, more Chinese will associate with each other and with non-Chinese on the basis of social or professional interest, but such non-kinship and non-locality gatherings will characterize the China-born scholars and professionals and their United States–born children more than they will the Chinatown-connected or Hawaiian Chinese. One indication for the latter observation is that nearly all of the participants in the Southern California Engineers and Scientists Association convention mentioned before were born, raised, and college educated in mainland China, Taiwan, and Hongkong.

Notes

1. It has been most brilliantly expounded by Ray A. Billington in *Westward Expansion: A History of the American Frontier* (New York, Macmillan, 1949), pp. 743–756.

2. Most American readers will probably say that Noah's parents had already died. I find Biblical indication that Noah's father did, indeed, die five years before the onset of the flood but his mother did not. The most important point is, however, that his parents do not figure in the flood episode at all.

3. Matthew 10:21. See also Matthew 10:34 and 10:35. It is perfectly true that contradiction to these is found in the Ten Commandments and elsewhere, but no sentiment even remotely similar to those of Jesus is expressed by Confucius and his followers. Furthermore, the principal anti-Confucian and antitraditional views appeared in China under the intense impact of the West.

4. If we count part-Chinese in Thailand, the estimates vary from 50 to 80 percent.

5. The central point here is not one of total emigration versus total nonemigration. All peoples have more or less migrated since the emergence of man. Certainly the Chinese were no exception. The Han Chinese came to today's China from somewhere in the Northwest. They moved forward slowly, first along the Yellow River valley and then pressed South. The area inhabited by Han Chinese became consistently larger. But the objective fact is that the Chinese, in spite of the great size of their population, have expanded far less within a much longer period of time than numerically smaller European peoples within a much shorter period of time. Having been bred in a tradition of the chosen men, individual separatism, and a history of world-wide colonial expansion, some Westerners either project the same motives into Chinese behavior or greatly exaggerate Chinese expansionism as justification for their own past sins or future designs. *China's March toward the Tropics,* by Herold Jacob Wiens (Hamden, Conn.: Shoe String Press, 1954), is one of these books.

6. China under the Nationalist government had ten additional provinces: Sinkiang, Ch'inghai, Ch'uan Pien or Inner Tibet, three provinces constituting Manchuria, and four provinces constituting Inner Mongolia.

7. See Francis L. K. Hsu, *Under the Ancestors' Shadow* (Stanford, Calif.: Stanford University Press, 1971).

8. A few Chinese have become missionaries for Western missionary organizations since contact with the West.

9. The three are (a) Tom Family Association, (b) Tan Kwang Yu Fang (Tom Quong Yee Fong), and (c) Chao Lun (Chew Lun) Benevolent Association. The membership of (a) consists of all persons bearing the surname Tan; that of (b) of all Tans belonging to one lineage; and that of (c) persons bearing four surnames of which Tan is one, each with the same radical (component) in common. There is a fourth association involving Tan people in San Francisco, Yu Chien (Yekon) Benevolent Association. I have not determined the basis for this separate organization.

10. In reality the number was five before 1862 and eight after about 1900 (See William Hoy, *The Chinese Six Companies* [San Francisco: Chinese Consolidated Benevolent Association, 1942], pp. 10–13). But we refer to it by its best known name, as do the administrators of the organization itself; a gilded plaque at the entrance to its San Francisco headquarters bears that same inscription.

11. Thus the Sze Yi (See Yap) group which separated itself from the Kong Chow Association in 1851 consisted of people from four of the six districts comprising the latter. Then in 1854 those members in the Sze Yi Association that hailed from T'ai Shan (Toy Shan, one of the districts making up Sze Yi) separated themselves and formed their own society. Finally, in 1862, members of the Sze Yi Association who belonged to Yin Ping (Yen Ping) district and others of K'ai Ping (Hoy Ping) district withdrew from it and formed a distinct entity of their own. The latter was named Ho Ho (or Hop Wo, United Harmony) District Association and it also drew to it all members of the T'ai Shan (Toy Shan) District Association who bore the family name Yee and all members of the Kai Ping (Hoy Ping) District Association who bore the name Ong. *The Chinese Six Companies, op. cit.,* pp. 2, 5, 12.

12. Some readers may consider this comparison illogical. However, this is because they are used to thinking of missionaries and at least some crusaders as being moral while the Mafia and tongs are thought to be immoral. But we might realize that the Mafia and the tongs (when they were actively engaged in crime), as well as missionaries and crusaders, are disturbers of the status quo; they are therefore considered troublemakers for the societies in which they operate. Thus both China and Japan had a history of resisting the intrusion of Christian missionaries. Independent India will not issue permits for entry of new missionaries. Was Carrie Nation, the founder of the Women's Christian Temperance Union not jailed on several occasions?

13. The Hung Men Hui, once a powerful secret society in Southern China which especially controlled the ports along the Yangtze River, did involve itself in Dr. Sun Yat-sen's revolutionary movement which toppled the Manchu dynasty and ushered in the first Republic. In fact, its branches and other tongs in the United States and especially in Hawaii made heavy financial contributions to Dr. Sun's cause. But the Hung Men Hui and its rival, the Ch'ing Pang, were always active at the local level, such as at a particular wharf in Shanghai. Neither had a national convention, even in secret. Their assistance to Dr. Sun was for the purpose of restoring the Ming dynasty against the Manchus. It is doubtful if they understood or were greatly in tune with Dr. Sun's revolutionary ideas about restructuring the Chinese society.

14. See Theresa A. Sparks, *China Gold* (Fresno, Calif.: Academy Award Guild, 1954), pp. 177–180.

Offerings to an ancestor during Ch'ing Ming.

Chapter Six

Religion

In discussing Chinese organizations, I have not touched on those rooted in religion; this is because the Chinese approach to religion is so fundamentally different from its Western counterpart that we must examine the subject separately in some detail. Religious differences externalized through affiliation to separate creeds, separate churches or temples, and separate rituals are as American as apple pie, as well as being Western, of course. Americans consider such differences to be part of the order of nature, for they occupy a major part of American life.

By extension, Americans—Jews, Christians, and nonbelievers alike—tend to regard strife due to religious differences as inevitable. There is hope for a utopia in which such strife is absent, but that portends the elimination of religion, a universal conversion to Christianity, or an ecumenical movement in which the different followers of Christ would agree to come together by emphasizing their similarities rather than their differences.

In contrast to this, religious differences have never meant much to the Chinese in China, who never engaged in religious quarrels. Consequently they have not produced any literature, theological or secular, explaining religious separatism or emphasizing religious unity.

Multiplicity of Gods

Simply defined, religion involves a system of belief in the supernatural, the activities based on that belief, and the results of those activities. All cultures in the world embody some such belief and the activities associated with it, but their patterns vary widely.

The Chinese believe in the existence of many gods, some more powerful than others, some more severe than others, with each god serving a different function. The Chinese God of War, who is also the God of Wealth, is very fierce; he will punish mercilessly those who do evil deeds. The Chinese Kitchen God and Goddess (his wife), on the other hand, are not martial at all. Their duty is to report to the Supreme Ruler of Heaven at the end of every lunar year the meritorious conduct or misbehavior of every household where they preside. The Chinese Earth God oversees the affairs of a locality; the Goddess of Fertility enables childless women to conceive; the Dragon God controls rain; the God of Agriculture blesses the crops; and so on, ad infinitum.

But all the gods, as well as the assistants and guards who help them discharge their duties, are equally true gods in Chinese thinking. There are simply no false gods. The notion that only "my" god is true and all other gods are false is a Western one which was central to Noah's thoughts in the Biblical flood myth; it is at the root of most Western religious disputes. Americans have inherited and amplified that belief whether or not they are churchgoers.

Chinese gods are, however, graded in a hierarchy, very much in the manner of the traditional Chinese government. Gods at a lower level can be bribed or fooled more easily than those at a higher level. In fact, noncorruptibility is a measure of a god's power and his exalted position. Chinese try to fool the Kitchen God and his wife in the same manner American children try to fool Santa Claus. They may have been bad all year long, but at the year's end, they display their best behavior just before the spiritual supervisors ascend to Heaven to report.

However, all gods may be powerful at some time for some things. After all, gods are supernatural beings and there is no sure way for man to be absolutely certain of their intentions. One can only try to be good and hope for the best. Since the behavior—especially the unspoken thoughts—of most human beings do not bear close scrutiny, the Chinese avoid becoming too intimate with any god.

There is a Chinese expression, "godly man," used in praise of powerful generals or particularly benevolent men of great renown. That expression refers to their earthly greatness, not to their ability to act in supernatural ways. Confucius expressed himself succinctly on this matter. A disciple asked him to explain gods and ghosts. The master replied, "respect gods and ghosts but keep them at a distance." The Chinese look askance at individuals who claim some god or gods are constantly with them.

The Chinese way in religion is nondivisive and nonexpansionist. One of the most difficult things for Western missionaries to explain to the Chinese is denominationalism. If there is one true God who created and loved all mankind, why should there be Protestants, Catholics, Methodists, Presbyterians, and even Northern and Southern Baptists? In the end, very few Chinese in China ever accepted Christianity, in spite of many armed invasions which led to Unequal Treaties with a provision allowing missionaries to go where they pleased. Some Chinese became rice-bowl Christians, but despite material lure in the face of poverty, by 1949 less than one percent ever became Christian, even nominally.

Lack of division makes expansionism unnecessary. Denominationalism necessitates expansionism; it cannot thrive otherwise. It requires that one resort to business tactics for the protection of one's belief in the supernatural. Competitors see the prosperity of one as the loss of the other. Therefore, each must think of ways of expanding his business. Each must advertise his wares aggressively and dispatch field representatives to obtain new markets. But while we have antitrust laws and a Food and Drug Administration to prevent unfair competition, false claims in advertising, and other malpractices within our own society, we have nothing to restrain religious "field representatives" (missionaries), especially in foreign lands.

Consequently, the history of Christianity within the West and of Western missionary intrusion into the non-Western world is replete with cutthroat competition among the different groups and orders. Many missionaries aligned themselves with native power structures when that alignment enabled them to make great conversion gains. The open antagonism between English Protestant missionaries and their French Catholic counterparts in the Royal Hawaiian days is but one of the many examples one could cite from all over the world. There is even evidence that Protestant missionaries incited Hawaiian riots against Catholics between 1827 and 1850.[1]

The Chinese attitude towards religion is nonexpansionist but inclusive. In the previous chapter we saw the Chinese lack of desire to proselytize. This lack does not emanate from a belief in many gods. The pre-Christian West also had many deities, but the Hebrew Kings, the Egyptian Pharaohs, and the Roman Caesars each had their favorite gods whom they tried to impose on their followers by the exercise of political power. No Chinese emperor ever attempted this.

The Chinese lack of proselytization is the result of the Chinese sense of inclusiveness vis-à-vis their gods. An old Chinese saying expresses this approach very well: *"Pu hsin shen pu hao chao t'a shen,"* which means "One must not be blasphemous toward gods in whom one has no faith." Over the centuries the Chinese attitude toward gods worshipped by other Chinese and non-Chinese peoples was marked by two characteristics. On the one hand this attitude was one of maintaining a respectful distance, which means they were not likely to say anything derogatory towards such gods or do anything to interfere with rituals sacred to them. On the other hand, the Chinese would not hesitate to include such foreign gods (including those worshipped by tribal peoples) in their temporary pantheon if the emergency was severe enough to justify it. A cholera epidemic was severe enough for Chinese in all parts of China to stage public prayer meetings at which they also appealed to Jesus Christ and Mohammed.[2]

Consequently, Chinese funeral spectators in or outside China could never have been the cause for the kind of uproar which marred the funeral of Fong

Ching (alias Little Pete). Fong came to this land at the age of ten and certainly made use of its opportunities. His legal and illegal operations made him a millionaire and the uncrowned King of Chinatown when he was barely twenty years old. A five-year prison term from 1887 to 1892 did not diminish his power and influence, but finally, in 1897, at the age of thirty-three, the hatchet men's bullets of a rival tong terminated his colorful career.

Little Pete's funeral was a funeral to outshine all Chinese funerals, but it was made a shambles at the cemetery by white spectators and memento-seeking women. Frank Norris, the top reporter of the *Wave*, a first-rate literary magazine in San Francisco was an eyewitness:

Perhaps I have seen a more disgusting spectacle than that which took place at Little Pete's funeral ceremonies, but I cannot recall it now. A reckless, conscienceless mob of about two thousand, mostly women, crowded into the Chinese Cemetery. . . . The women thronged about the raised platform and looted everything they could lay their hands on: China bowls, punk, tissue paper ornaments, even the cooked chickens and bottles of gin. This, mind you, before the procession had as much as arrived.

The procession itself was rather disappointing—from a picturesque point of view. . . .

At the cemetery, however, things were different. There was a certain attempt here at rites and observances and customs that would have been picturesque had it not been for the shamelessness, the unspeakable shamelessness, of the civilized women of the crowd.

Suddenly the coffin arrived, brought up by staggering hack drivers and assistants, a magnificent affair of heavy black cloth and heavy silver appointments. The white women of the crowd made the discovery that Little Pete's powder-marked face could be seen. They surged forward in the instant. The droning priest was hustled sharply. He dropped his little bell, which was promptly stolen. The mourners on the mat, almost underfoot, were jostled and pushed from their place, or bundled themselves out of the way, hurriedly, to escape trampling.

Just what followed after this I do not know. A mob of red-faced, pushing women thronged about the coffin and interrupted everything that went on. . . . A mounted policeman appeared and was railed at. . . . There can be no doubt that more ceremonies were to follow, but that those in charge preferred to cut short the revolting scene.

The coffin was carried back to the hearse, a passage at length being forced through the crowd, and the Chinese returned to the city. Then the civilized Americans, some thousand of them, descended upon the raised platform, where the funeral meats were placed—pigs and sheep roasted whole, and chickens, and bowls of gin and rice. Four men seized a roast pig by either leg and made off with it, were pursued by the mounted police and made to return the loot. Then the crowd found amusement in throwing bowlfuls of gin at each other. The roast chickens were hurled back and forth in the air. The women scrambled for the china bowls for souvenirs of the occasion, as though the occasion were something to be remembered.[3]

Under no circumstances would the Chinese have done what these white Americans did. They would not have been so insensitive to other people's grief. But above all, they would not have been so disrespectful toward the soul of any dead, and they certainly would not have cared to make personal mementos of articles offered to the dead or used at the funeral. The Chinese would not have been guilty of any of this conduct because they have been trained to regard any ritual as having a validity of its own and to hold all varieties of supernatural belief to be equally true.[4]

Of course, white racism might have played a part in the unforgivable crudity on the part of the spectators at Little Pete's funeral. Yet the behavior at Little Pete's funeral reminds me of similar conduct at the funeral of Michael Todd, with Elizabeth Taylor as the mourning widow, half a century later at a cemetery in Chicago. I am curious to know how wealthy Little Pete's wife and mother could have become by selling his life story and personal belongings, either actual or manufactured, in the way the mother and wife of Lee Harvey Oswald, President Kennedy's assassin, are still enriching themselves today. But, then, Little Pete and his relatives were not so Americanized or wise to American ways.[5]

Organization and Persecution

In economics we hear of the laissez-faire and competitive economy of capitalism as contrasted to the controlled and planned economy of totalitarian states. I cannot help but observe that the Chinese have a way of dealing with religion more in line with the capitalist spirit in contrast to that of the Americans which is more characteristic of the totalitarian.

For example, the Chinese have never been interested in organized religion. Westerners in general, and students of religion in particular, have frequently mistaken church organization with religion. That is only natural. Proceeding from the notion that not only is there one true God but only one view of that God, namely one's own, Western men of religion naturally worry about the question of "who is and who is not with me." Once that difference becomes important, the assumption that those who are not "with me" are "against me" is inevitable. Consequently, Western man finds it necessary to make sure that the number of those "with me" increases and increases. Organization is an indispensable tool in making sure of who is "with me" and in adding members to "my" religious club—either church or temple.

It is therefore scientifically baseless to indicate, as have so many writers and students of China, how many Chinese in China are Buddhists, Taoists, or Confucianists. The Chinese approach to religion is first and foremost a personal matter. If someone I care for is sick and the doctor's medicine has not helped, of course I am going to make some offerings at a temple and pray to the gods for assistance. But if, in spite of the offerings, the patient's condition does not improve, I shall certainly be open to suggestions as to which other gods in other temples are known to be more efficacious. When I hear of better healers should I not go to them in all haste?

The Chinese approach to temples and gods is not unlike our modern-day approach to stores. Some Americans prefer the Jewel supermarkets and others the Red Owl supermarkets. If they are dissatisfied with both, they may switch to National Tea stores. We have no reason to classify Chinese into Buddhists or Taoists any more than we can classify Americans into Jewellians or Red Owlists. It is as absurd as that. The Chinese temples have no records of memberships; they have no membership drives. They welcome all who want to come and pray; they never turn anyone away because of color of the would-be worshipper's skin. When they need money to renovate or to build, they look for a few wealthy backers whose names and contributions then head the list of their public appeal. They accept money from anyone and they may never see many of their contributors again. This is because many Chinese regard contribution to the building of a temple, or a pagoda in it, as an act to increase one's other-worldly merit; once established, the merit will remain forever.

For these reasons, the Chinese have not only shown no urge to proselytize but have had no history of religious persecution. It is true that some scholars have called attention to the so-called persecution of Buddhists in the T'ang dynasty; but this is a misinterpretation of the facts.

A few T'ang emperors persecuted Buddhists, not because they hated Buddhism as a false faith but because of their suspicion that treasonable elements were using monasteries and monkhood as a temporary refuge.[6] Accordingly, the persecution took three forms. First, the monasteries, temples, monks, and nuns were to be registered and subject to inspection. Second, even in the most notable Great Persecution of A.D. 845–846, the emperor merely reduced the number of temples and monks to be allowed in the two national capitals and the prefectures but did not eliminate them. There was no inquisition or witch-hunting, two types of persecutory activity which characterized the West. Finally, the emperor destroyed all temples in excess of the decreed number and defrocked all monks and nuns other than those allowed to keep their vows.

When we consider the prolonged and bloody religious persecutions of the West, it is remarkable that the Chinese rulers achieved their end without resorting to execution or imprisonment, and that the T'ang persecution was short-lived and was never repeated. In my view, intensive and extensive persecution requires not only persecutors but also people who invite persecution as well, because of their commitment to particular faiths.[7]

Kinship and Religion

How did the Chinese develop their particular way in religion? We can no more answer that question than we can another: how did Westerners develop theirs? We know that as early as the myth-making time of Noah, Westerners already had their one-God view of religion, and Americans have definitely inherited the same view from their European ancestors. The Chinese, too, already had their "respect gods and ghosts but keep them at a distance" view of religion when the man-centered story of Yu and the flood was formed.

We do know how the two diverse ways of religion are continued and escalated within the two peoples from generation to generation. The central psychological and social arena for human development everywhere is the family and its extension, the web of kinship.

An American individual, as he grows up, must learn how to be independent of not only his parents but the other members of his wider kinship group. Although extremists reject their parents with some vehemence, most young people equate maturity with the ability to be independent of one's parents and kinsmen and develop personal autonomy. But no individual can really be totally independent of all other individuals. One who breaks away from parents and kinsmen must, as surely as the sun rises, seek the company of other human beings in fraternal organizations, political cells, cause-promoting clubs, and proselytizing churches.

The signs of a Chinese individual's growth and maturity do not include independence from or rejection of parents and kinsmen. In fact, his development includes finding better ways of serving his parents by greater insight into their wishes and more familiarity with his place in the wider kinship web of cousins, uncles, and in-laws and his duties and obligations within this web. Having been so deeply woven into a human network which comes with his birth, the Chinese individual has far less need than his American counterpart for intimacy with a particular god or with those who share the same views about his gods, exactly as he has less need to champion a particular cause or combine with those who are likewise devoted.

Consequently, the Chinese traditionally treat monks and priests with equal distance. It was not uncommon for many Chinese homes in China to have a sign on their outer gates reading: "Sheng Tao Wu Yuen (literally, "we have no predestined relationship with monks and priests" but simply, "no monks and priests"). The religious functionaries are hired to perform rituals when needed but they are outside of regular society and they cannot serve as centers of human bonds.

In the previous section we noted the difference between the short-lived and regulatory nature of religious persecution under the T'ang emperors and the widespread and annihilative nature of religious persecution throughout the history of the West. But persecution of certain individuals or groups by public authorities tells only part of the story. Were that the only source of religious persecution, a change of policy at the top and a new government fiat would eliminate it. We know this is not the case.

Religious persecution in America is a grass roots matter. When jobs and the right to live wherever one can afford are denied to people because of their church affiliation or religious ancestry, that is religious persecution writ large. When parents interfere with their children's romance and marital plans because they disapprove of interfaith marriage, that, too, is religious persecution writ large.

It was such widespread individual attitudes and acts which led masses of Americans to drive Mormons out of the East and Midwest. Such people continue to nurture in our country a latent anti-Semitism and discrimination against atheists. There are still repeated efforts by Protestant supremacists to force the institution of prayer in public schools.

Religious persecution by public authorities did not flourish in China because it enjoyed no grass roots support. Since the Chinese assign to their relationship with family and kinship a much higher priority than to their connection with gods and temples, they have never allowed religion to be the divider of men.

Nor should the reader be surprised to find the really universal religious creed among the Chinese is the Cult of Ancestors. Chinese in different parts of the country vary in their actual observance of rites to ancestors, but no Chinese denies or argues about it. The entire complex—including funerals, graveyards, clan temples, genealogical books, and periodic offerings (including the offerings of whole roasted pigs and sheep at the funeral of Little Pete, which so amused the White spectators)—is not strange to any Chinese.

A people who maintain such permanent links with their ancestors and anticipate a continuation of these links with their yet unborn descendants tend to have little time and enthusiasm for alliances other than those with family, kinship, and locality. Their social self-sufficiency reduces their need for causes both honorable and dishonorable, for gods, and for joining with other human beings in clubs or groups to promote causes and particular brands of theology.

Religion among the Chinese in America

A visitor to the Chinese cemetery in Manoa Valley of Honolulu during the month of March will see it bustling with activity, especially on Sundays. In front of graves both new and old are clusters of Chinese men, women, and children paying homage and making offerings to their dead. The offerings may be slim or abundant, including pigs and chickens roasted whole or simply sliced meats and plates of fruit. But cups of alcohol are poured on the ground in front of the tombs, bundles of burning incense placed before them, and large or small quantities of specially made paper money and papier-mâché life-like figures are burned for the benefit of the dead. The entire assemblage kneels down in twos and threes to kowtow to the dead. There are always offerings of flowers. And finally, in front of many of the tombs, a large string of firecrackers is exploded. A notice posted at the entrance to the cemetery indicates that the City of Honolulu has given special permission for the use of firecrackers between the hours of 9:00 A.M. and 5:00 P.M. during the Chinese *Ch'ing Ming* period when it is the custom for all Chinese to *sao mu* (literally "to sweep the graves" of their dead).

In the center of this Chinese cemetery, on a high point, can be found the grave of a Chinese bearing the family name Wong. The inscription on the stone is already so weather-beaten as to be illegible but it indicated that he was the earliest Chinese settler in the Islands. He used to be referred to as *hsien chu* (earliest ancestor) and lately *hsien yu* (earliest friend). He left no descendants, but on one Sunday each March visitation and homage with magnificent food, wine, and paper money offerings are made by a large group of males, sometimes several hundred. The leader of this group is the current President of the United Chinese Benevolent Society, and the other participants are representatives from many different Chinese organizations. The ceremony is topped off by the explosion of a giant string of firecrackers. During the entire *Ch'ing Ming* period, offerings of food and incense will be made to the tomb of this *hsien yu* more or less continuously by other Chinese as individuals or families.

The ritual patterns in Honolulu have somewhat deviated from their counterparts in China. For example, it is a Chinese custom of long standing to have a picnic at the cemetery right after the offering is made. Usually some of the offerings are left on the graves or burned with the paper money, but most of them make up part of the picnic. The Hawaiian Chinese no longer have such a picnic. Those who have a meal together following the visitation will drive back to one of their homes and have refreshments there. The Chun-Hoon brothers, sisters, in-laws, and children, for example, hold this lunch at one of their supermarkets. It is also a Chinese custom of long standing for women to wail at the graves of the newly dead; this is no longer observed. And, of course, there are no clan cemeteries.

In spite of these modifications, all of the ritual activities at the Manoa Chinese cemetery are recognizably Chinese. While some Chinese in Hawaii go to the graves on a Sunday for convenience, other Chinese still look up the current year's Chinese almanac before deciding on the date and time of the visitation. Everything else involved is Chinese. What prevails among Hawaiian Chinese is more or less found on the United States mainland among Chinatown-centered Chinese.

However, some Hawaiian Chinese are bona fide members of Christian churches. According to Reverend Charles Kwock of the First Chinese Church of Christ and Harold Jow of the United Church of Christ, two churches with predominantly Chinese congregations, and Father Dever of the Catholic Diocese, the total number of Chinese Protestants in Hawaii is somewhat less than 4,000, about equally divided between those belonging to churches with predominantly Chinese congregations and those without, while the total number of Chinese Catholics is estimated at 8,000 to 10,000. There are no Catholic churches with predominantly Chinese congregations anywhere in Hawaii. Also, while there are no reliable estimates of the number of church members among Chinatown-centered Chinese in the mainland United States, it is doubtful that more than 20 percent of them (about the same proportion as in Hawaii) are so affiliated.[8]

Some of these Chinese Christians have departed to a great extent from the traditional Chinese ways. For example, several second- and third-generation Chinese have entered Catholic monasteries as priests and nuns. One son of the Assistant Police Chief, Clarence Liu, was ordained in 1970 and another son is studying to become a priest. For Chinese parents in China, celibacy for both sons means total discontinuity of their family line, a fact they find hard to accept.

Another man, Mr. C. K. Ai, a first-generation immigrant to Hawaii who became a Christian while a student and later became a millionaire, ordered something most unusual for a Chinese. His first wife died very young; his second wife bore him eight children and lived until her 80's. Mr. Ai died ten years later. Before his death, he asked that his ashes be divided into two equal parts to be buried with the remains of each wife. Thus, today, there are only the tombs of the two wives with no separate tomb for the husband. The descendants of Mr. Ai do not visit the graves of their forebears during the traditional *Ch'ing Ming* period and do not perform the traditionally Chinese rituals when they do go. Instead they celebrate Easter, Thanksgiving, and other traditionally American occasions and on these holidays they visit the graves of dead relations but offer flowers and silent prayers only.

Mixing of Religions

Most Chinese Christians in America are not exclusive in their views of and participation in ritual activities. Twenty years ago I made the following observation on religion among Hawaiian Chinese:

Two ... facts are to be noted in this connection: (1) it is a rule, rather than an exception, for members of the same family to have different religious affiliations, such as, for example, a Catholic father, a Methodist son, and an Episcopalian daughter, while the mother retains her custom of worshipping at Chinese temples. (2) Differences in religion do not seem to hamper Chinese family solidarity. Frequently, Christian Chinese have told me that if and when their mothers ask them to go to Chinese temples they do everything the elders request. They do not see any conflict with their own church activities.[9]

Twenty years later, and after another sojourn of twelve months in Hawaii, I find no reason to change this observation. Furthermore, my acquaintance with a variety of Chinese in mainland America during the last two decades has convinced me that what I said about the Chinese in Hawaii at that time is still valid for Chinese–Americans as a whole, even including the scholars and professionals.

As a rough approximation, I would guess that not more than one third of the scholars and professionals of Chinese extraction are Christian; some are only nominally Christian. Many of them came from missionary universities in China. But denominational differences and even differences between Christians and non-Christians have never been of significance in business, social relations, or even as a topic of conversation. I do not know of one case in which church affiliation was a serious obstacle to marriage or a reason for hostility between parents and children. Among my hundreds of Chinese friends and acquaintances, I literally do not know who is and who is not a Christian, and even less, who is a Methodist or a Unitarian.

Except for church-sponsored or -connected events, no Chinese meeting begins or ends with a prayer. The Midwest Chinese Student Alumni Service, located in Chicago, was begun by the organizational energies of a retired missionary from China, but as time went on, the tendency was to reduce rather than increase the church influence on its activities. At one time a Chinese Catholic priest attempted to set up a rival Chinese student organization, but that floundered for lack of support. For the last several years, the Kuomintang, or Nationalist Party of Hawaii, a purely political entity, has held its officer installations, with firecrackers and lion dances, at the clubhouse of the Hawaii Chinese Buddhist Society.

The manner in which Chinese religious functionaries speak about their different temples is another indication of this laissez-faire attitude. There are, for example, two major Chinese Buddhist temples in Hawaii. One is linked with the Chinese Buddhist Association of Hawaii and the other to the Hawaii Chinese Buddhist Society. Two more or less different groups of Chinese support them; like all Christian churches, each group can boast of some well-known figures. However, the monks tell me that while there are two different temples, there is no dissension in theology between the two temples. "Buddha is the same; and all gods are the same."

Earlier we described the ritual activities at the Manoa Chinese Cemetery. But if one visits the Pauoa Christian Cemetery (an old Chinese cemetery) during the same period, one does not see any of those rituals. Instead there is more of the usual type of observance common among white Christian Americans such as flowers and silent prayers on Easter, Memorial Day, Christmas, birthdays of the dead, Father's Day, Mother's Day, and so on. However, it is typical of the Chinese that some Christians are also buried in the same Manoa Chinese Cemetery, as well as the newer Nuuanu Cemetery, with the non-Christian Chinese. Many non-Christians honor their dead on Christian holidays; many Christians, on their part, retain Chinese ways in addition to Christian customs. For example, some Christians give a big dinner on the anniversary of the death of their father or mother, according to the conventional Chinese custom.

Perhaps most revealing of the Chinese idea of religion is the fact that the Chinese in America and in China do not have a term comparable to "heathen" or "pagan." Chinese Christians simply do not entertain the attitude of superiority towards non-Christians which is so common among Western Christians. During a recent visit to a Chinese cemetery where the usual Chinese offerings were being made to the dead, I met several Chinese professional men, one of whom was a Christian. They knew of my interest and discussed some of the ritual details with me. On separate occasions two of them said, "You know, I am kind of embarrassed to be seen by *haole* [White] friends when we do this," referring to the food and paper money offerings.

The average Chinese, whatever his ritual observances, usually feels little or no defensiveness towards other Chinese. He knows that he will not be an object of disapproval or contempt whether or not the spectators share his customs. On the other hand, he is only too aware of the hauteur with which the average white American reacts to religious views and activities different from his own.

At this point the reader will recall the incident which was related earlier in which the California widow's daughter and daughter-in-law stood between her and her grandchildren because they did not want any more proselytization. Is this case, perhaps, one in which religious affiliation appears to be stronger than family ties, and therefore evidence in contradiction to what we have outlined here?

My answer to this question is, at first, a positive one. But then we must observe that her situation is rare among the Chinese in America and, more importantly, that she and her children have not broken their relationship because of this quarrel. There was tension and dissatisfaction on all sides but, as we noted before, they arose because the ameliorating circumstances of the purely Chinese social context were absent. The real question is, will the American way in family and kinship gain strength among the Chinese in America? If so, will most Chinese in America ultimately let church affiliation be a divider of men, too?

While I agree that more changes in the Chinese pattern of family and kinship are eventually inevitable, I think such changes will proceed more slowly among the Chinese than among most other minority groups in America. Furthermore, I do not think the direction of those changes will be wholly in the Western model. However, as the human relationships supplied by the family and the wider kinship net weaken and dissipate, church affiliation or other differences will certainly hold the possibility of becoming more relevant to the Chinese.

The logic of our analysis leaves no other alternative unless we can redefine Americanization and consciously seek a design for encouraging minority groups like the Chinese to contribute something of their family and kinship patterns to the cultural melting pot of the majority. That task will not be easy, but we shall examine its merits and feasibility in the last chapter of this book. In the meantime, we must turn to another aspect of Chinese life in America, namely friendship and related matters.

Notes

1. See Francis L. K. Hsu, *Americans and Chinese: Purpose and Fulfillment in Great Civilizations* (New York: Natural History Press, 1970), Chapter 9.

2. See Francis L. K. Hsu, *Religion, Science, and Human Crises* (London: Routledge and Kegan Paul, 1952).

3. Quoted by Richard H. Dillon, *The Hatchet Man: The Story of the Tong Wars in San Francisco's Chinatown* (New York: Coward-McCann, 1962), pp. 338–339.

4. The anti-missionary riots in nineteenth century China were not a Chinese counterpart of this American episode. The nineteenth century rioters were reacting to the foreigners who came to their land as conquerors and destroyers of their way of life. Little Pete and his people were doing none of that.

5. I realize that Oswald's widow was Russian born. But that is less important than the fact that the American public continues to buy such things and that she was willing to let his memory be so used.

6. There is also the possibility that some emperors resented the wealth amassed in some monasteries. But since the T'ang emperors' actions were not repeated by rulers of later dynasties, this possibility must be discounted.

7. For a fuller discussion of the question, see Francis L. K. Hsu, "Chinese Kinship and Chinese Behavior" in Ping-ti Ho and Tang Tsou (eds.), *China in Crisis,* Vol. 1, pp. 579–608. Chicago: University of Chicago Press, 1968.

8. In 1968 about 20 percent of San Francisco Chinese were members of Christian churches according to *A Study of Chinese Churches* (Berkeley, Calif.: Bureau of Community Research, 1968), p. 26. Dr. Kenneth A. Abbott tells me that "in the 50's and the 60's, the number of Chinese Christian churches multiplied rapidly in the San Francisco Bay Area (reflecting the national trend). A far greater number of Chinese come into contact with churches as youths and retain a vague feeling of connection later." (Personal communication.)

9. Francis L. K. Hsu, "The Chinese of Hawaii: Their Role in American Culture," *Transactions of the New York Academy of Sciences,* Series II, Vol. 13, No. 6 (April 1951), p. 244. The only statement which I must revise now concerns an error in estimation. I said then that "practically all Chinese born and raised in Hawaii in recent years have become Christians." The fact is that Chinese membership in all Christian churches in Hawaii never exceeded about 20 percent of the Chinese population in the Islands, an estimate we noted before. There has been no large increase during the last two decades.

A Chinese dinner party.

Chapter Seven

Friendship
and Hospitality

In Taiwan newspapers in recent years, I often read articles, comments, and short notes on the subject of *jen ch'ing wei* which, for want of a better translation, means roughly "the feeling of intimacy among human beings." A few of these were written by white American students who had attended Chinese universities or had completed a period of research; more were written by Chinese who have had some experiences with foreigners.

The most important theme these writers wanted to convey was the fact that Chinese, in contrast to Westerners, are much warmer toward and more solicitous of other men—foreigners or natives. They are always ready to help and they are willing to spend time and energy to confide in or sympathize with others or to be the object of such confidence or sympathy. Their hospitality is fuller and more genuine than that of Americans. I have known cases of American students who cannot wait to return to Taiwan because they love its human warmth.

However, at least one American student wrote to complain that he was not taken into the inner circles of his fellow Chinese students. He felt that he was constantly left out. He did not see the *jen ch'ing wei* others talked about so much. He thought it was more appearance than reality.

In line with this minority opinion are two or three articles by Chinese students and professionals who said they experienced far more friendliness in the United States than they ever did in Taiwan.

One example the latter group points to is the behavior of the Taiwan bus conductors (women as a rule) compared with American bus driver-conductors (men as a rule). The former are generally rude and callous toward passengers in contrast to the business-like courtesy of the latter. In fact, these Chinese students and professionals point out that some American bus drivers go out of their way to be considerate, such as giving advice about routes or opening the door for a late passenger even though the door had just been closed and the bus was about to proceed.

Another example Chinese writers have dwelt on more than once is the road courtesy of American motorists which sharply differs from their Taiwan counterparts' lack of it. They recounted how passing American motorists had generously helped them when they were out of gas or had flat tires and how such experiences had never been heard of in Taiwan.

One reason for such conflicting views may be due to the fact that motoring is not part of Chinese culture and therefore is not included in traditional Chinese rules of behavior. This exclusion is repeated elsewhere. For example, high-caste Hindus may work side by side with Untouchables in factories today, but will refrain from socializing with them. Factories are of recent Western origin and the Hindu pollution rules do not, therefore, apply. People all over the world make that kind of situational separation in their attitude toward fellow human beings and things.

Another reason for such conflicting views is undoubtedly differential perception, which in turn depends upon the observer's previous experiences. Anthropologists have noted that contradictory reports of American visitors to Soviet Russia seem to be related to their itinerary. Those who went to the provincial areas of Russia first and then to Moscow were much more impressed by Russian life than those whose itinerary was the reverse. But in spite of the hazards of observation, there are important cross-cultural differences in the patterns of interpersonal relations. The interpersonal relations we shall examine at some length center in friendship.

Friendship in General

Among human beings, friendship is a universal institution, whatever the nature of the society and culture. Even some animals become friends with each other; we know this from our experiences with dogs and cats. The beginning of friendship occurs when two or more individuals with no prior connection develop good feelings toward each other and are drawn together. The basic ingredients of friendship entail a wide spectrum of activities: from physical contact, sharing, secrets, hospitality, gift-making, mutual assistance, all the way to exchange of greetings and Christmas cards.

Anthropologists have observed that all human societies possess some rules governing the treatment of strangers. An offer of food and lodging is usually part of that treatment; the exchange of gifts is another. The Eskimo custom of temporary wife-sharing with a guest has gained a great deal of attention because it is so different from the usual patterns to which most of mankind adheres; but in the framework we have discussed, it is merely a form of gift-making—albeit a bit too generous for the taste of the rest of the world. However, for most peoples of the Far East, kissing in public as a way of expressing friendship between persons of opposite sexes is spectacularly distasteful. That is why older generations of Far Easterners thought of Westerners as generally loose in sexual morality. But in our framework, that custom is merely a form of friendly physical contact.

Friendship is often built on top of other existing human links. Thus one employee may become more friendly with a few fellow employees in an office or factory which hires hundreds or thousands; or one cousin may become more friendly with a few cousins than most others. In such a case, friendship serves as a double agent of human cohesion or it may become an impediment to other duties and obligations. For example, employees friendly with each other are likely to cooperate better as a working team than those who are not. But a cousin who favors some cousins because of friendship is likely to be resented by his other cousins who feel they deserve his solicitude and help by virtue of their positions in the common kinship structure.

Social Baggage versus Psychic Baggage

The nature of friendship and its manifestation vary from culture to culture. Previously we noted the great importance of family and kinship relationships for the Chinese individual, as contrasted to the desire on the part of the American individual to be free from them. This is not to say that most Americans do not want to start families and kinship relationships of their own. However, they want to be freed from those ties which they grew up with and, although they may not like it, they anticipate that their children will do the same.

For the Chinese, family and kinship take precedence over friendship. His first obligations are determined by his position in that human network. Outside of family and kinship, the next level of importance is given to his ties with his local community. The extent of the latter may include an entire province and therefore be quite large, but his link with the province does not negate his place in a village, a subdistrict, and a district which is a unit of the province.

Since the preexisting network of human ties has priority over others, the Chinese individual is not as free as the American individual to move away from it; and when and if he does, it is equally difficult to form entirely new associations without reference to the old ones wherever he may be. In other words, he cannot freely decide to commit himself to objectives and activities without reference to his duties and obligations vis-à-vis his preexisting ties.

The Chinese individual faces the wider world with a large piece of social baggage, but a relatively small piece of psychic baggage. His social baggage is large because he is a component of a large human network, has an inalienable part in it, and must make future decisions in the wider world according to its dictates. His psychic baggage is small because he is never alone, has no need to reach maturity by way of rejecting parents and kinsmen, and can call on them for help without losing his self-respect. There are many human beings with whom he can share his happiness and his miseries.

The American pattern is for the individual to enter the wider world with little or no social baggage. That is, he struggles to free himself from the parental yoke and from any suggestion of dependence on it. Even before he is capable of actual independence, he has already made symbolic demands and gestures along that line. To achieve self-respect he must make a world of his own, find his own friends, and acquire his own identity. In fact, identity crisis is common and such a crisis is often used as an explanation of erratic and delinquent behavior on the part of youth.

Consequently, although the American individual faces the wider world with much more of a free hand socially than the Chinese, he is psychically more burdened. A culture pattern in which self-reliance is emphasized generates psychic stress on the part of children as well as their parents. The young will be touchy in manufacturing and guarding signs of independence just as the old will find it hard to relinquish their de facto control. The greater the pressure of the young for a break, the greater the need of the old to maintain the connection. Hence we have domineering fathers, "Jewish mothers," Huckleberry Finns, and rebellious children. People who have to resort to rebellion to be free cannot but carry that rebellious chip on their shoulders. Individuals who have to make it on their own cannot help but be beset with a good deal of insecurity when faced with a sea of equally vociferous peers.

Two Patterns of Friendship

These contrasting personal burdens act powerfully in shaping two different models of friendship. When the Chinese individual meets those outside the family, kinship, and local area, his first impulse is to bring them into his primary network, or to seek links with them in formal or informal arrangements according to kinship or locality models. Thus for the Chinese, friendship tends to intensify rather than replace kinship and locality ties. Even in Hawaii, Chinese children still tend to address their parents' close friends as "Auntie" or "Uncle" regardless of race.

For the American, friendship dilutes and replaces kinship ties. In fact, even between parents and their minor children, the ideal link is friendship and not kinship. For example, many readers must have seen the television serial, "My Three Sons." In one of its episodes the widower father was suffering from a bad case of nerves just before his wedding. His three sons presented him with a pre-wedding gift engraved "To our best friend, our Dad." The message and the obvious delight on the face of the father would have been baffling or at least irrelevant to the average Chinese in China. They would have interpreted the incident as evidence that the sons wanted to create a distance between themselves and their father because a stepmother was on the way.

However, it is impossible for most Chinese to be associated with other human beings on the basis of kinship and locality bases alone. The Chinese in America especially have to meet and work with non-Chinese as schoolmates, employers and employees, co-workers, neighbors, fellow church members, and occasionally participants in the same causes.

My view is that even when the Chinese cannot structurally incorporate—according to the kinship and locality model—the people they come into contact with, they still tend to react and relate to them on the basis of attitudes inherent in Chinese relational content. All human relationships possess two aspects: structure and content. The former has to do with the role or roles each individual plays with reference to another. The husband–wife relationship is such an arrangement wherever a man and a woman are accepted by their society as being married. The same is true of arrangements which make people fathers and sons, leaders and followers, ministers and members of congregations. However, content refers to the attitudes embodied in the structure, and it can vary greatly within the same structural relationship.[1]

For example, although the same monogamous husband–wife relationship is found in Japan and in America, the attitudes of the spouses toward one another in the two societies differ widely. For one thing, compared with their American counterparts, Japanese wives generally show far more deference toward their husbands. For another, most Japanese husbands entertain their business associates and friends in restaurants in the evening where their wives are never present rather than entertaining them at home.

One feature which distinguishes the Chinese attitude toward friendship, in China as well as the United States, is its nonconcern with the element of authority. Americans, because of their imagined or real history of struggle to free themselves from their parents, are prone to find it difficult to live with unequal friendships in which one party is more wealthy than the other, more beautiful than the other, or more clever than the other. For example, in spite of their proverb, "A friend in need . . . ," Americans are very wary of extending a helping hand to friends who are down. The friends they have helped are later likely to resent having revealed their worst and pull away. A Chinese is less likely to mind giving to or receiving help from friends. The Chinese benefactor has no worry about resentment on the part of the object of his generosity. On the contrary, the friend who has benefited will probably be openly grateful for life and seek to repay him even more generously in the future.

Closely linked to this attitude is the tendency of Chinese friends to enter into what Americans would regard as each others' private affairs. For example, Chinese often settle disputes by seeking the intervention of the disputants' friends. Chinese are not only fond of match-making for friends but also like to settle family quarrels.

My wife and I have had bad experiences in the latter regard in spite of our understanding of the differences in culture pattern. Normally my wife and I follow the American pattern in dealing with white friends; we mind our own business. But not long ago a couple to whom we were devoted were on the verge of separation. He was in misery because he was the unwilling party, and the victims would have been four small children ranging from age three to ten. We knew we should not have become involved, but then we thought perhaps this was an exception since our friendship was of long standing and they seemed to understand something of the Chinese philosophy. We tried our best to talk to them singly and together on social occasions. The result: soon after we saw her she locked him out of their house; a little later she filed for divorce; and she has since told others that she resented our meddling, though he has retained his friendship with us.

Two other features of Chinese friendship must be noted: inclusiveness and continuity. The first has to do with the Chinese tendency to expand kinship-like relationships, a fact we noted in connection with the Chinese custom of dry-parenthood. A Chinese sees nothing wrong with his best friend having another best friend, or with the parents or brothers of his friend tending by extension to become his friends. Chinese friendship, like Chinese kinship relationships, tends to be additive while its American counterpart tends to be one of replacement, in the same way that marital ties replace parental ties for both spouses.

The other feature, namely continuity, refers to the relative permanence of Chinese friendship in comparison with friendship among white Americans. The Chinese like to look up old friends while Americans tend to do so mainly through class or combat unit reunions. For the Chinese in America, an outstanding contrast is the brittleness of American friendship. A common Chinese reason for maintaining a friendship is the "oldness" of that friendship. "I've got to see him because he is such an old friend" is often heard among the Chinese. On the other hand, "We no longer see each other because we no longer have anything in common" is a well-known expression among Americans. When specific interests are the basis for friendship, that friendship is bound to shift and terminate with much higher frequency.

Friendship and Sexuality

We must ask why American friendship is so shallow and so brittle. If, as we noted before, the individual has to seek human associations outside of family and kinship because his culture does not allow him permanency within them, does he not want to substitute relatively durable friendships for it? The answer is to be found in the American fear of homosexuality because his culture is preoccupied with diffused sexuality. In contrast, the Chinese lack this fear because their culture assigns the sexual aspect of man to specific areas.

A man and a woman meet, they have a romance, become engaged, marry, and raise children; these are specific areas where sexuality is either explicit or implicit. The same thing must be said about a man visiting a house of prostitution. The difference between the two situations is that whereas sex is part of a larger social context in the former, it is the main object in the latter. That sexuality is involved in both is undisputable. That is the limit of the Chinese view of sexuality.

The American view of sexuality includes the above areas but it spreads elsewhere and seems to be confined by no boundaries. Sex appeal may be associated with automobiles, found in the persons of political candidates, and attributed to church ministers—just as it can be achieved through the use of certain deodorants, toothpastes, and cigarettes. The extent to which the American tendency may go may be gauged by the following episode, which many readers will undoubtedly agree is not unique.

A white American historian and his wife spent a year in Taiwan, during which time the wife became extremely fond of the *yu t'iao,* or Chinese equivalent of a doughnut. It has the same coloring; it is shaped like two giant cigars about eight to ten inches long bound together. In the course of an after-dinner conversation this lady expressed such enthusiasm for it that she was asked to explain the article, since her listeners were white and had never tasted them. She fumbled for words for some seconds and then began, "It is very sexy, you know!"

As a child in Manchuria, as a student in Shanghai, Peking, and other towns, or as an adult working, sojourning, and studying in many provinces of China, I found *yu t'iao* to be ubiquitous; yet I never heard anything that would remotely suggest a link between *yu t'iao* and sex. The lady's remark came as a total surprise to me. But then she is so much more American than I am, and the pattern of her projection is quite in tune with the American culture.

Being equipped with well-defined boundaries for sexuality, Chinese even in America usually appear to white Americans to be impassive or at least nondemonstrative and reserved. The extreme American stereotype of the Chinese is "inscrutability." The Chinese are certainly not without expression and feelings. It is just that, in comparison with Whites, their manifestations are so much milder and pass unnoticed by their exaggeratedly expressive white observers. But the well-defined boundaries of sexuality gave the Chinese their capacity for forming deeper and therefore more lasting friendships with members of the same sex than white Americans. They do not have to fear homosexuality.

Consequently throughout the centuries, deep and lasting Chinese friendship bound together old men and young men, employers and employees, and even persons of drastically different social statuses, such as peasants and scholars. And Chinese scholars have immortalized lasting friendship in poetry and prose, of which the following is but one of many examples:

A Visit
by Wang Chien (T'ang Dynasty, 618–905 A.D.)

Over our cups of wine
In the arbor by the stream
We talked and talked
Until it seemed
As if we had left no subject
In all the world, from east to west,
Untouched.

And now my cart has rumbled off,
And when I turn my head
To see you once again,
You are lost to sight, old friend,
Hidden
By the autumn rain.[2]

This pattern of Chinese friendship has continued and in fact escalated in Taiwan. The Taiwan dailies, especially the Literary Supplement of the *Chung Yang Jih Pao* (*Central Daily News*), are replete with prose and verse eulogizing, or emphasizing devotion to, or expressing deep sorrow over, the loss of the writers' parents, employers, employees, teachers, comrades in arms, or just friends.

By contrast, Americans, being products of a culture where sexuality is not confined by externalized boundaries, are certainly very demonstrative and unreserved where heterosexual associations are concerned. The extreme Chinese stereotype of the American is a fun-loving sexually immoral individual. Here, too, the fact is not that Americans are truly without sexual morality, but in comparison with Chinese, the differences are so great that they tend to overshadow the fundamentals. However, if the Chinese will look closer, he will discover that although Americans tend to be much freer with persons of the opposite sex, their relationship with persons of the same sex, under cover of easy conviviality, is much more constricted than the Chinese. The camaraderie consists of a powerful handshake, ready banter, fast acquaintance, and unfulfilled promises. The restrained nature of American friendship among persons of the same sex is spectacular in its lack of sentimentality and the absence of psychic intimacy.

This American tendency is even different from that of Germans, who are but another variant of the West. The German–American, Kurt Lewin, a social psychologist, noted the differences as follows:

Germans entering the United States notice usually that the degree of friendly and close relation, which one may achieve as a newcomer within a few weeks, is much higher than under similar circumstances in Germany. Compared with Germans, Americans seem to make quicker progress towards friendly relations in the beginning, and with many more persons. Yet this development often stops at a certain point; and

Chapter Seven

the quickly acquired friends will, after years of relatively close relations, say good-by as easily as after a few weeks of acquaintance.[3]

Superficially this reflection might well have been made by a visiting Chinese about Americans. But that is only part of the reality. What Lewin saw was merely a difference in degree. German friendship begins more slowly than its American counterpart, but once begun, the friends tend to communicate a great deal more of their inner selves to each other and the relationship has more of a lasting quality to it.[4]

However, compared with the Chinese, both Germans and Americans guard their autonomy and privacy with too much zeal. Furthermore neither Americans nor Germans are able to give sentimental expression to a friendship between members of the same sex as freely as the Chinese. The free-flowing sexuality has enabled Americans to enrich and liven up their view of the world of men, gods, and things with a variety of erotic or near-erotic projections. The Oedipus complex, the apple and original sin, and the virgin birth are but the outstanding examples which they have inherited, accepted, and amplified. But the same flowing sexuality has prevented American men from forming deep and lasting friendships with other men, and, by equalitarian extension, women with women.

Thus, while Americans of opposite sexes daily come closer to complete public exhibition of their sexual ardor for each other, Americans of the same sex must observe increasingly rigid taboos against lasting fraternization with each other in the absence of the other sex or of other common goals for conquest such as business or war—to be noted below—and especially against any sort of physical contact. Americans have produced practically no poets who have left us lyrics on devotion between males.[5] (Nor have the Germans.)

In a search through European literature, I find three well-known examples concerning friendship between males: two love poems by Paulinus of Nola;[6] "Lycidas" by John Milton;[7] and In Memoriam by Alfred Tennyson.[8] The poems and other communications between the teacher, Ausonius, and his pupil, Paulinus, were unashamedly those of ardent lovers through the agony of separation. They were expressions of late Roman times (about the end of the fourth and the beginning of the fifth centuries after Christ), when love between males was still totally acceptable. The other two poetic works, one in the seventeenth century (Milton) and the other in the first half of the nineteenth century (Tennyson), proceeded from deep personal friendship into abstract theological and philosophical speculations. Henry Van Dyke says of the ninth and last division of In Memoriam:

This is a stronger, loftier song than the poet could ever have reached before grief ennobled him; and from this he rises into that splendid series of lyrics with which the poem closes. The harmony of knowledge with reverence; the power of the heart of man to assert its rights against the colder conclusions of mere intellectual logic; the certainty that man was born to enjoy a higher life than the physical, and that though his body may have been developed from the lower animals, his soul may work itself out from the dominion of the passions to an imperishable liberty; the supremacy of love; the sure progress of all things toward a hidden goal of glory; the indomitable courage of the human will, which is able to purify our deeds, and to trust. . . .[9]

This pattern of abstraction from the personal to larger issues is equally evident in "Lycidas." In fact, Milton was not even a personal friend of the subject of his poem; he was expressing the grief of a third person. Milton then used this imagined grief as a vehicle to express his pessimistic attitude toward the evil times on which poetry had fallen as well as to attack the corruption of the clergy. Even this manner of going from the personal to the abstract in conveying feeling for a dead friend is rarely found in American poetry.[10]

On the other hand, American novelists have not failed to convey something of the American taboo against male intimacy. Two examples will suffice.

One is found in John Steinbeck's *Of Mice and Men.* As the reader will recall, this is a story of Lenny and George, two itinerant laborers who worked from plantation to plantation. Lenny is physically powerful but mentally retarded. George is devoted to him and protects him like a brother. When they arrived in the men's dormitory of the farm where the fateful killing eventually takes place, the other laborers at once become curious about the relationship between the two newcomers. They hurl a barrage of questions at the two and smile knowingly when George admits that he and Lenny have been together for a long time. The author leaves no doubt in the mind of the reader as to what the inquisitors knowingly smiled about. To them, a homosexual liaison between Lenny and George is obvious.

The other example comes from J. D. Salinger's *Catcher in the Rye* in which the hero is an adolescent named Holden Caulfield. After being dismissed from his prep school in Pennsylvania for misconduct, Holden roamed the streets of New York because he felt diffident about going straight home to his parents and giving them the bad news. He hated most of his fellow students and all of his teachers except one, to whose New York apartment he therefore repaired. The teacher and his wife were very kind and put him up for the night in their living room. The next morning, as Holden awoke from his sleep, he realized that his teacher was sitting beside the couch patting his head. Thereupon Holden shot out of his teacher's apartment like lightning. The reader never meets the older man again in the novel, but if he is American or knows something of the American taboo, he cannot miss the meaning of Holden's precipitous exit. Since Holden was an adolescent, his reaction was intense, but he was merely exaggerating the American norm of fear of homosexuality.

Friendship and Business

Since American males cannot get close to each other through friendship, they have to meet and deal with each other on other grounds. The most serviceable of these is business. They can pursue not only pleasure or adventure, but wealth as well. And they turn pleasure and adventure into a business or business-like enterprise.

The characteristics of business are that the parties involved must be useful to each other, have calculable rights and obligations in common resources and rewards, and achieve tangible results. They will cooperate with each other as long as their common enterprise pays dividends, and they can each go their separate ways without attachment to the old partners if or when it fails. This is what we mean by business is business, or business and pleasure do not mix.

Thus, lack of depth in friendship has motivated Americans to give greater impetus to success in business or business-like enterprises, but the emphasis on business or business-like relationships has tended, in turn, to further dilute human links between parents and children, between spouses as well as between friends.

The Chinese culture is one in which friendship (or kinship and marital links) takes precedence over business. It requires that the individual do his best to fulfill his duties and obligations according to the former relationship at the expense of the latter undertaking. This was the *jen ch'ing wei* that some Americans in Taiwan became so enthralled by and many Chinese in Taiwan write and talk about as a most valuable asset of the Chinese way of life. This is also the source of the Taiwan parents' complaints we discussed before. They are dissatisfied because their sons and daughters in America have decided to reverse the priorities, so that the business principle is more important than the kinship and friendship principles.

When a whole society and all its major government functions are run on the kinship and the friendship principles, that society cannot achieve modern statehood, and public enterprises cannot fulfill their promises. Nepotism and corruption will necessarily eat away their foundations. But when the business principle becomes so supreme that all human beings turn into calculable units of production, then most people cannot help but converge towards what David Riesman called "the lonely crowd."

A Bifurcated Adjustment

The Chinese in America may be said to have made a series of bifurcated adjustments between the two ways of friendship. A few of them have entirely subscribed to the American side of the equation while many older people in Chinatowns and Hawaii have made no adjustment at all. The former think or consciously hold the view that there is no difference between Chinese and non-Chinese. The latter have no non-Chinese friends; in fact, they have little or nothing to do with American-born Chinese or with Chinese of the scholars and professionals group. This is one kind of bifurcation. A second type of bifurcation is for the individual to maintain two sets of associations, each with more or less distinct rules. Most Chinese in America seem to follow, knowingly or otherwise, the latter model. Second- and third-generation Chinese in the scholars and professionals group who have not been raised in Chinatowns or Hawaii tend to begin, because of the pull of peers, by seeing no difference between themselves and Whites. As they grow older, however, the different expectations of the Whites and of the Chinese they meet will necessarily lead them to revise their views. Then they, too, tend to fall in with the dual-association model, however, unevenly. Two other kinds of bifurcation will become clear below.

Following the dual-association model, a Chinese has the following seven alternatives:

1. Business relations with Whites but friendship with Chinese;

2. Friendship with Whites but business relations with Chinese;

3. One set of business relations and friendship with Whites and another set of the same with Chinese;

4. Business relations with Whites but business relations and friendship with Chinese;

5. Friendship with Whites but business relations and friendship with Chinese;

6. Business relations and friendship with Whites but only friendship with Chinese;

7. Business relations and friendship with Whites but only business relations with Chinese.

Thinking about the Chinese as a whole, I find most who follow the dual-association model take alternatives 3, 4, and 1, in that order of popularity. And nowhere can the different rules be more clearly seen than in hospitality.

For example, traditional Chinese dinners are more abundant and offer more variety than American dinners. Therefore, when Whites do not reciprocate in kind, most Chinese simplify their fare for non-Chinese guests. But since offering such simplified fare runs the risk of offending their Chinese friends, most Chinese in America tend to entertain Whites and Chinese separately.

We then have two sets of manners. If the guests are White, the hostess will not urge her guests to eat more, the dinner fare will be ample, cocktails will be served, the table set in more or less the meticulous fashion of American formal dinners, the number of guests exact with no children present, and the conversation will tend to be orderly with its noise level relatively low so that most, if not all, guests can hear each other. On the other hand, if the guests are Chinese, the hostess will urge her guests repeatedly to eat more, the dinner fare will be abundant consisting of many dishes, the tables (usually several, including bridge tables) will have no more than a simple cover and some chopsticks, the number of guests will be somewhat fluid, and there usually will be children; occasionally cocktails of some kind are offered, but most Chinese do not drink, and the conversation tends to be chaotic and loud, sometimes near shouting pitch, for there are several sets of conversations and cross-conversations.

However, other than this dual-association model, two other kinds of bifurcation are visible. For a majority of Chinatown-centered Chinese, hospitality to family members and close relatives tends to be different from that offered to other Chinese. For one thing, traditional abundance marks the former while a more subdued fare marks the latter. Also, two decades ago, a visiting Chinese of some distinction to Hawaii or any mainland Chinatown would have been overwhelmed with invitations, as he still is in Taiwan today. But the present tendency is that he is likely to feel the lack of *jen ch'ing wei* among his expatriates.

The separation between friendship and business is a bifurcation I consider of most importance. It possesses the greatest significance in terms of the success of Chinese in American life.

As we noted before, the Chinese way in friendship intensifies kinship bonds. Friendship expands and continues in the kinship model. Both kinship and friendship have priority over business considerations. That was the basic source of traditional China's organizational weakness in society and government. That was why large-scale and impersonal enterprises could not arise and could not function. It is a weakness which the new government in mainland China since 1949 has been trying to eradicate with drastic and often cruel measures.[11]

The Chinese in America have found a social context in which they can reverse the priorities without the ordeal of a Communist Revolution. They live and work among a majority of Whites whose cultural standards stipulate that business calculations must take precedence over kinship and locality ties. They are in an eminently advantageous position to bifurcate their lives: for success in business and industry they do not mind being members of the "lonely crowd," but for interpersonal intimacy and warmth, they still can find something of their age-old *jen ch'ing wei* within the webs of kinship and locality.

Notes

1. For a more complete discussion of the difference between structure and content, see Francis L. K. Hsu, "Structure, Content, Function, and Process," *American Anthropologist* 61 (1959), 790–805.
2. T'ang dynasty. Reprinted from *Poems of the Hundred Names* by Henry H. Hart, p. 130, with the permission of the publishers, Stanford University Press. Copyright 1933, 1938 by the Regents of the University of California. Copyright 1954 by the Board of trustees of the Leland Stanford Junior University. The Chinese have many poems concerning the pleasures of meeting friends, sorrow and parting, or death of friends.
3. Kurt Lewin, *Resolving Social Conflicts* (New York: Harper & Row, 1948), p. 20.
4. *Ibid.*, pp. 20–25.
5. Ralph Waldo Emerson wrote one poem, "Friendship" (1841). Joseph Parry has a poem that sounds like Chinese: "Make new friends, but keep the old; those are silver, these are gold."

6. Helen Waddell, *Medieval Latin Lyrics* (London: Constable & Co., 1929), pp. 34–7.

7. *The Complete Poetical Works of John Milton,* a new text edited with introduction and notes by Harris Francis Fletcher (Boston: Houghton Mifflin Co., 1941), pp. 116–20.

8. *In Memoriam,* Michael Davis, ed. (London: Macmillan Co., 1960).

9. Henry Van Dyke, *The Poetry of Tennyson* (New York: Charles Scribner's Sons, 1905), pp. 149–150.

10. I have found two modern examples: Stephen Spender's "One More New Botched Beginning," in *Selected Poems* (London: Faber and Faber, 1965), pp. 79–80; and Ted Walker's "Elegy for a Trotliner," in *The Solitaries: Poems, 1964–1965* (New York: George Braziller, 1967), pp. 53–54.

11. For fuller discussion of this, see Francis L. K. Hsu, *Americans and Chinese: Purpose and Fulfillment in Great Civilizations* (New York: Natural History Press, 1970), Chapters 14 and 15.

Mr. Bill Way, a wealthy Chicago businessman who prefers to live in Chinatown.

Homage to earth from China. In the mound is a patch of earth from the ancestral
home of the Chuns in China.

Offerings to an ancestor during Ch'ing Ming.

"The King and I," Chinatown, Chicago. (Photo by Harry Tun.)

Homage to the tomb of the first Chinese in Hawaii (*hsien chu* or *hsien yu*) during Ch'ing Ming.

Chinese–American troops who have just received first aid treatment are seen in a 2½-ton truck for transfer to the far rear, where they will receive hospital care. Taken during World War II. (Property of EB, Inc.)

A student outing in San Francisco. (Photo by Victor Wong/BBM.)

Chapter Eight

Adolescence

A San Francisco-based political reporter writing in *The Atlantic* about young immigrants from Hongkong to San Francisco says:

> To the horror of a Chinatown that believes in self-discipline, a number of these teenagers, perhaps 300, have become rebels, dropouts, runaways, street loiterers, petty thieves, even violent agitators. It was inconceivable to Chinatown that Chinese youth would adopt the public obscenities of the militant blacks, or join college demonstrations in the Third World Freedom Movement. When they did, it was blamed on a "Communist" plot.[1]

The reporter explains the phenomenon by the fact that "today's Chinese arrivals, unlike their forefathers, come determined to be Americans," but not having been properly prepared or forewarned, they find their conditions of existence terribly disappointing, especially in contrast to what they assumed, under the pressure of parental aspiration, before arrival.

Among other things, this article shows that delinquency or nondelinquency is not a matter of biological heredity. Rather its probability is to be sought in human circumstances and how these circumstances affect the decisional trends of the individual. Given the right combination of conditions, most adolescents will not seek delinquency as an outlet. What, then, are the human conditions bearing on the adolescent in the Chinese social context?

Continuity versus Discontinuity

There are several factors favoring delinquency, one of which is discontinuity in experiences as the individual moves from childhood onwards. For example, being reared first in great affluence and then suffering deprivation is one kind of discontinuity. Little or no discipline in childhood and strong restrictions afterwards is another form of discontinuity. If one has been trained to take the helm of a large corporation and then finds he has to settle for employment as a mechanic, that is yet another kind of discontinuity. Finally, if the sons are expected not only to do better than their parents but also to be different from them, that is also a matter of discontinuity.

Generally speaking, the Chinese traditional society and culture have the effect of continuity of experiences. In the first place, although parents want their children to do better than they have done, most elders will be happy to see just the preservation of what they already have achieved. *Ch'eng yeh* describes a man who has initiated success on his own, but *shou yeh* refers to a man who has not squandered away the success of his father, and the latter is also highly respected.

The worlds of children and adults, then, are not as strongly separated in the Chinese context as they are in the American context. For example, as soon as it is physically possible, Chinese children tend to accompany their parents much more than American children do. Previously we noted that one characteristic of Chinese hospitality is the probable presence of children at dinner parties for adults. That is one way to generate continuity rather than discontinuity between the generations. But the difference goes farther. Chinese parents, having the philosophy that children should be ushered into adulthood as soon as is practicable, tend to share the vicissitudes of their own lives with their children, in happiness as well as in misery.

Chinese children are always present at adult functions, including weddings and funerals. Erik Erikson relates the case of a white American child given to convulsive attacks who told the therapist about his puzzlement by the sudden disappearance of his grandmother from the house. He was told by his mother that Grandmother went on a long trip and did not have time to say goodbye to him. Then when he saw and asked about a giant box being carried out of the house, he was told it contained his grandmother's books, although he did not recall that Grandma was such a prolific reader, nor did he see why an assemblage of relatives shed tears over a box of books. What really happened was that the grandmother had died but the child was never told the truth.[2]

This case might have been a bit extreme, but shielding children from unpleasant happenings of the adult world is as accepted an American pattern as it is untrue to the Chinese scene. The more affluent the parents, the more they will try to protect their children. Chinese children, even in America, tend to be initiated into the world of their parents imperceptibly. By the time they reach adolescence they already have a fair appreciation of the intricacies and difficulties of life that their parents have had to contend with all along.

Consequently, as they grow up Chinese youngsters experience far less that sharp conflict between the ideal and the real. As children, their world has never been greatly insulated from that of adults. They do not expect it to be made of sweetness and light, in which all the good are rewarded and all the bad are punished. Instead, they already possess a social maturity commensurate with their physical capabilities.

Nonexclusive Parental Control

Early, gradual entry into the adult world is one set of factors encouraging continuity. Another set comes from the fact that Chinese parents, because of the nature of their family and kinship patterns, tend to have nonexclusive control over and supervision of their children. Chinese kinship and other relationships tend to be inclusive rather than exclusive. That is why, as we noted before, children's friends tend to be friends of their parents and "dry son" relationships lead to "dry siblings" and "dry grandfathers." Chinese uncles and aunts are surrogate parents whether the real parents wish it or not. Chinese parents tend, therefore, to be less touchy about advice from other quarters concerning their children. I have never heard of Chinese parents, in China or in America, resenting the disciplinary actions of schoolteachers.

Consequently, Chinese children do not see their own parents as the only benefactors of their needs, or the only stumbling blocks to their freedom. For even if they can overcome or circumvent parental restraints, they have a wider kinship or pseudo-kinship network to contend with.

Chinese parents, on their part, tend to feel less threatened than American parents by the maturation and independence of their children. The sense of continuity works both ways. Children have less need for a sharp break from their parents, and parents have less need to hold on to them. For Chinese, human relationships tend to be additive rather than of a replacement type.

The Role of Peers

The tendency for continuity between the generations in the Chinese context has lessened the need of the adolescent to seek affiliations with his peers, just as the discontinuity between the generations in the American context has increased it. All human beings must relate to other human beings. That is a universal fact, in spite of some who wrote so glowingly about the value of solitude, including Thoreau. If these writers really cared about solitude, they would not have written so much about it. What they really wanted was to start clubs of solitude lovers. What differentiates peoples in different societies and cultures is not the need for affiliation, but the variations in intimacy and in purpose of such affiliations.

The Chinese tendency is to maintain affiliation with kinship or at least to carry on the spirit of that affiliation throughout life. In contrast is the American pressure to sever the parental link, at least psychologically, and to avoid subordinate roles or at least dream throughout life of working for oneself.

The Chinese, therefore, not only has less need to seek nonkinship affiliations, but when and if he does, he is likely to seek not only horizontal ones but vertical ones as well, while the American must seek nonkinship affiliations and also must shun vertical connections in favor of horizontal connections. The individual who has to depend upon horizontal relationships must make greater exertions than those who chiefly deal with superiors or inferiors since parents can be taken for granted but peers cannot. Parents in all societies tend to express affection for their children even when the youngsters are ungrateful. But no peers anywhere have great love for each other; they certainly cannot take each other for granted. Because they compete with each other for the same things, each must be continuously on the lookout for trouble with others, trouble which might lead to rejection.

The American adolescent is therefore likely to be under the tyranny of his peers far more than his Chinese counterpart. This condition compels the former into greater anxiety dictated by his needs for maintaining or improving his status in his peer group. In defense of that anxiety, he must conform to its demands which may include not only overt signs of flaunting parental wishes and injunctions, but also violent gestures, including immoral acts and even murder and mayhem as well.

To the extent the Chinese kinship pattern will change under the impact of American conditions, Chinese teenagers in the United States will not, of course, be exempt from such developments. But the fact is that Chinese adults in America, as we have seen before, have not given themselves greatly to nonkinship and nonlocality organizations, and are not known for their cause-promoting or -suppressing efforts. Some Chinese college students and professionals have organized themselves into fraternities and sororities in the American model, but there is absolutely no evidence that such organizations enjoy a high prestige among Chinese Americans comparable to their place among white Americans.

The Nature of the Wider Society

In America the most desired position of the individual is a combination of (a) economic and social independence, (b) successful and rapid achievement of this goal, and (c) the use of creative means in achieving an identity of one's own.[3]

Economic independence demands holding a job to one's liking and cessation of parental financial assistance. That achievement in turn helps the individual to establish social independence—which includes, among other things, full control of one's own hours, movements, and activities as well as the creation of a conjugal unit on one's own terms.

Rapid success is an old American ideal. Nothing expresses this sentiment better than the proposal by Grayson Kirk, former President of Columbia University, to shorten our college education from four years to three, and the enthusiastic and favorable comments this proposal has received from the public.[4] Although college presidents in particular and society in general have been kept too busy during the last decade by student unrest and black violence to put this proposal into effect, the shortening of the time needed for securing a "union card" (the B.A. diploma) to the high achievers' club is a step that will not be far off. The increasingly lowered age of dating is one indication of the same trend. The proliferation of youth at the executive level of corporations is another.

The American emphasis on creativity is also undeniable. To be described as being creative is the highest form of praise an American can hope for; to be branded noncreative is his worst damnation. But when success is the principal goal and competition is severe, the emphasis on creativity has given men license for indiscriminate and irresponsible use of any means to pursue an end. When adults do their best to reach ends without regard to the means, the high standards preached in society tend to become a mockery to the youngsters.

By contrast, Chinese society—whether before or after Western contact—does not encourage individual independence and frowns on cutthroat competition for individual ends. In traditional times, the individual worked to continue and add glory to his ancestral line. After the 1911 Revolution, but especially since the 1949 Communist Revolution, he has been enjoined to transfer his kinship-oriented goals to the larger aims of saving the ancestral country (*chu kuo*) and reviving and augmenting its historical greatness. Furthermore, having been gradually initiated into the ways of adult responsibilities and pitfalls at an early age, the Chinese adolescent is less confused; he therefore feels less frustrated than his American counterpart vis-à-vis the adult world. Being inalienably enmeshed in his kinship network, he is also more insulated from its pressures. There is simply less reason for adolescent turbulence in the Chinese social context.[5]

At this point the reader may call my attention to the much reported Red Guards and wonder if they do not represent a serious departure from what I have described so far. My answer is that the Red Guards are new in goals and in methods, but they have not departed from the Chinese notion that the individual is part of and must serve the larger whole. In traditional China the individual was trained to serve his family, wider kin group, and community in that order. On the other hand, Republican China, especially Communist China, called upon him to serve his nation as a whole. The Red Guards were initiated by one faction of the state against another, and the Red Guards acted by and large under the belief that they were patriots trying to save the country from ruin. How else could we explain that the Red Guards came and left with such equal suddenness? Can the United States government eliminate juvenile delinquency or call off its antiestablishment forces so easily?[6]

The Changing Chinese Adolescents

It is not my thesis that the Chinese adolescent is, by nature, immune to delinquency or violence. What I wish to underline is that his human network, the pattern of culture, and the larger society in which he matures, have combined to reduce such a probability. When and if significant changes occur in this combination of circumstances, what can we expect from the Chinese adolescent?

In view of the history of discrimination and ghetto existence of Chinatown-centered Chinese in America, it should be obvious that many a young Chinese man or woman—both native-born and immigrant—has experienced great frustration and trauma as he strove for a life better than that of his elders. Possessing no literary background, these Chinese, and even the Hawaiian Chinese, have produced but scant expression in the written word. A few short life histories collected by sociologists reveal their difficulties and how they felt about them.[7] Recently I came upon a collection of 70 poems, of which the following is one, by a young man who came to America in the early 1920's.

When I Left for America

When I left for America, my tongue could scarcely move
To say "Goodby" to my mother;
Tears fell from my eyes, and my heart was wounded. I suffered.
My friends stood on the wharf waving their hands and hats;
The great ship blew a horn, then sailed out to the deep.
I stood on the upper deck and saw my friends grow smaller and smaller,
In a moment, I saw only the sky, the ocean, a few seabirds flying.
I met, on the boat, strangers—not one of whom I had known before—
Among them, a man and a woman, talking and smiling;
But I do not know what I said to them; the sound of the words were
        quite different from that of my accustomed voice.
I was lonely; I wished that I might return home.
I remembered what my friends had told me;
"In a few years we hope to see our dear friend,
The great hero, come home with new knowledge,
To help our country and our people."
I have lived in America six years,
I have not gathered much of anything
To satisfy these expectations.[8]

The circumstances and sentiments in this poem are typical of a sojourner. He came to America to make good, and he hoped to return to help China when he had succeeded. He obviously found his life in the New World unsatisfactory, lonely, and frustrating. But not one of the poems expresses antiestablishment sentiments. Instead, the young poet sings praises of the beauty of nature, philosophizes about life, remembers his mother and sister in China, reflects on

New Year's Eve in China and the United States, speaks of personal disappointment in love, and expresses sorrow for the unfortunate fate of friends, children, and beggars.

He is keenly aware of racial discrimination. But he simply expresses his feelings in a poem entitled "Brotherhood" which puts the burden of division into races on God and ends with the lines:

> Each is the same before birth,
> And each is the same dust when dead.[9]

At times he must have been in the deepest despair. But he only calls on God for help as he expresses himself in a poem called "In the Dark" which ends:

> Why is there not any place for me?
> Open the gate, oh God! Show me the way! [10]

Even when he laments the miserable life and death of his good friend, he does not blame American society. Instead he says:

> He fought long years for life,
> For his daily bread.
> He, a Chinese, died in a strange land.
> In a little room where he lodged.
> No one knew, for a day, of his death.
> Then the landlady knocked at his door—
> She found him dead. . . .
>
> For seven years he worked throughout this land
> Doing good for others, not for self.
> But now they speak with kindly words;
> Yet offer not their hand.
> No one! No one!
> They care not whether he be dead or yet alive.
> He knew so many persons,
> But he had none as friend.
> Buried in a lonely grave,
> He is gone! His work is finished!
> He has found his true Church;
> He knows his true Friend;
> He is with his true God.[11]

We have no knowledge about what became of this young Chinese immigrant, but we can fairly guess that he was among those Chinese whose conduct earned them the white praise of being the most law-abiding in the land. He came to America to find the fulfillment of his ambitions and when he did not find that fulfillment, he did not blame the society. Instead he blamed himself, he lamented fate, and he comforted himself with thoughts about nature, about his relatives in China, and about the fact that all men are equal when they are dead.

However, that was in the 1920's. China and·the Chinese who have come to the United States since World War II are a far cry from what they were half a century before. China herself has undergone a total revolution which, though it created colossal misery among some sections of the population, has given the Chinese everywhere, however vicariously, a new antidote to their century of humiliation and inferiority vis-à-vis the West. Many of the Chinese who left China—for Hongkong, Taiwan, and America—because of the Revolution are no longer imbued with the view of life of our poet, Mr. Lum. Instead they, too, tend to pursue individual happiness as their fellow immigrants from Europe have done for many decades and to demand equality in that pursuit. In this process many of them have been additionally propelled by the fact that they are separated from their main kinship links in China. They came as permanent settlers, not as sojourners.

Over and above these forces is the fact that most of the Chinatown-centered Chinese and Hawaiian Chinese are now third-, fourth-, and even fifth-generation Americans. Many of them have been educated and elevated from the humble status of their forebears. Although they have not as a whole given themselves to militancy as a way of gaining their ends,[12] they are obviously not ignorant of alternatives other than those which passed the minds of our poet Lum and other Chinese who came at his time.

America and Americans who meet the Chinese are also very different from those of the 1920's. To the great credit of some of our legislative and administrative leaders and many well-meaning citizens, our laws have been revised so that race is no longer a bar to immigration and citizenship. But the liberalized societal framework has unfortunately sharpened the division between those who labor for the realization of the ideal of equality and freedom and those who see no salvation except White supremacy, Protestant supremacy, or some other kind of inequality.

America is a society in turmoil, in which many groups are divided against themselves (Christians, Southerners, Northerners, businessmen, and labor) or against each other (Blacks against Whites, tenants against landlords, the people on the right against those of the left, and youth against the establishment). The issues are sometimes mixed and the battle lines are often confused, but a general dissatisfaction, a sense of social malaise, and strong feelings that something should be done either to hurry the clock forward or to turn it backward are undeniable. In the eyes of the new arrivals from the Far East, that former grand spectacle of an all-powerful, progressive, idealistic, and peaceful white America is no longer so imposing or at least not so unified. They can still find more opportunities and better material conditions of existence, which is why they still come. But along with such chances for self-improvement they see a good many cracks in the American armor.

Thus a combination of circumstances has created, for the Chinese adolescent in America, a very different social and cultural context than that which was known to those preceding them. The effect of the new context is that in contrast to the early Chinese immigrants, he is more sophisticated in American ways than his forebears,[13] and he can find more Whites of varying persuasions who share his aspirations and with whom he can ally himself. He can also afford to be less dependent upon his kinship and community ties for any sort of support than the first Chinese immigrants. But the content of Chinese kinship (see Chapter 7) is still strong enough in his psychosocial orientation so that, as yet, not more than a fraction of Chinese adolescents have joined the ranks of pot-users or delinquents or antiestablishmentarians.[14]

Notes

1. Mary Ellen Leary, "San Francisco's Chinatown," *The Atlantic,* March 1970, p. 42.

2. Erik Erikson, *Childhood and Society* (New York: W. W. Norton & Co., 1949), p. 27.

3. As we shall see in Chapter 10, being American consists of more than this, but this is, I think, what most Americans present to the world and to themselves.

4. Grayson Kirk (as told to Stanley Frank), "College Shouldn't Take Four Years," *Saturday Evening Post,* March 26, 1960.

5. This lack of adolescent turbulence is not an unmitigated blessing. If each generation follows exactly in the footsteps of the last, little or no social progress can be expected. The generation gap often means the challenge of the opportunistic old by the idealistic young. That is the very seed of internal impetus for a better world. For a fuller discussion, see Francis L. K. Hsu, *Americans and Chinese: Purpose and Fulfillment in Great Civilizations* (New York: Natural History Press, 1970), Chapter 13.

6. For a fuller discussion of this and other developments in China see Francis L. K. Hsu, "Chinese Kinship and Chinese Behavior," in Ping-ti Ho and Tang Tsou, eds., *China in Crisis,* Vol. 1 (Chicago: Chicago University Press, 1968), pp. 579–608.

7. One such collection was assembled by Dr. Robert E. Park of the University of Chicago from 1924 to 1929 as part of his study of race relations on the West Coast. See *Orientals and their Cultural Adjustment,* Social Science Source Documents, No. 4 (Nashville: Social Science Institute of Fisk University, 1946), mimeographed. About half of the documents pertain to the Japanese.

8. Chung Park Lum, *Chinese Verse* (New York: Lop Quan and Co., 1927), pp. 111–113.

9. *Ibid.,* p. 89.

10. *Ibid.,* p. 133.

11. *Ibid.,* pp. 161–163.

12. The Chinese Red Guards in San Francisco are still a minor phenomenon. However, some Chinese youngsters in their frustration are bound to be influenced by the example of Blacks. More recently tension has arisen between some Chinatown-centered Chinese in New York City and the telephone company. The latter has purchased a 272-unit tenement apartment building in the Chinatown area with the intention of tearing it down and replacing it with a skyscraper office building. Many tenants, having been forced to move out, are now having second thoughts. Some of them hold the view

that they should forcibly reoccupy the building, just as has been done by some other ethnic groups and poor Whites. But the *Chung Kuo Shih Pao* (*China Times*), published in New York City's Chinatown, counsels negotiation for better terms and improvement rather than force (*The China Times,* October 5, 1970).

13. For some systematic evidence through psychometric tests bearing on this point, see Stanley L. M. Fong, *The Assimilation of Chinese in America: Changes in Orientation and Social Perception,* M.S. thesis (San Francisco: San Francisco State College, 1963), unpublished.

14. Mrs. John Israel calls to my attention the fact that since the immigration law of 1964, thousands of Chinese have come to the United States to join relatives already here. "They constitute a group less easily absorbed than the China-born professionals, less sophisticated in American ways than their American-born cousins, and often too old to learn English easily, scorned by the Chinese–Americans as F.O.B.'s (Fresh off the boat); they have begun to create a delinquency problem. My sister, who teaches junior high school English has a special class of these newcomers and finds them very hard to reach." (Personal communication.) Mrs. Israel's assumption here is that those who are hard to reach are likely to be delinquents. I cannot agree with that assumption although I realize this group needs special attention.

And he went for that heathen Chinee

Engraving reproduced courtesy of the Library of Congress.

PLAIN LANGUAGE FROM TRUTHFUL JAMES

Bret Harte

Which I wish to remark,
  And my language is plain,
That for ways that are dark
  And for tricks that are vain,
The heathen Chinee is peculiar.
Which the same I would rise to explain.

Ah Sin was his name;
  And I shall not deny
In regard to the same
  What that name might imply;
But his smile it was pensive and child-
  like,
As I frequent remarked to Bill Nye.

It was August the third,
  And quite soft was the skies;
Which it might be inferred
  That Ah Sin was likewise;
Yet he played it that day upon William
And me in a way I despise.

Which we had a small game,
  And Ah Sin took a hand:
It was euchre. The same
  He did not understand;
But he smiled as he sat by the table,
With the smile that was childlike and
  bland.

Yet the cards they were stocked
  In a way that I grieve,
And my feelings were shocked
  At the state of Nye's sleeve,
Which was stuffed full of aces and
  bowers
And the same with intent to deceive.

But the hands that were played
  By that heathen Chinee,
And the points that he made,
  Were quite frightful to see—
Till at last he put down a right bower,
Which the same Nye had dealt unto me.

Then I looked up at Nye,
  And he gazed upon me;
And he rose with a sigh,
  And said, "Can this be?
We are ruined by Chinese cheap labor,"
And he went for that heathen Chinee.

In the scene that ensued
  I did not take a hand,
But the floor it was strewed,
  Like the leaves on the strand,
With the cards that Ah Sin had been
  hiding,
In the game "he did not understand."

In his sleeves, which were long,
  He had twenty-four packs—
Which was coming it strong,
  Yet I state but the facts;
And we found on his nails, which were
  taper,
What is frequent in tapers—that's wax.

Which is why I remark,
  And my language is plain,
That for ways that are dark,
  And for tricks that are vain,
The heathen Chinee is peculiar—
Which the same I am free to maintain.

Chapter Nine

Prejudice

When the son of Dr. Ralph Bunche, a Negro and a Nobel Peace Prize winner, was not allowed to become a member of the West Side Tennis Club of Forest Hills, New York, and the fact became known through the press, everyone recognized it for what it was: a case of discrimination because of racial prejudice.

Since the early 1950's, all sorts of movements, laws, and administrative measures have come into being to combat this kind of prejudice. The Black Panthers, the SDS (Students for a Democratic Society), the Supreme Court school integration decisions of 1954 and 1970, the Fair Employment Act, the school bussing measures: these and many others have as their principal aim the legal elimination (or at least the amelioration of the deleterious effects) of racial discrimination in housing, occupation, and education.

On television, however, we hear daily body counts and see burning villages, and we read about and see published pictures of atrocities against civilians, including women and children—all in Indo-China. These are usually attributed to the Viet Cong or North Vietnamese, but many Americans have some doubt about the identity of their perpetrators. It is true that there are many American protesters who want the United States to pull out of Vietnam without further delay, but there are also many Americans who see Asian sufferings as necessary because their white protectors wish to prevent Vietnam from turning Communist, even by way of democratic elections, for they profess to know what is best for Asians. Many Americans continue to believe, and some American newspapers and columnists repeat the myth, that Asians do not place the same value on human life as Americans and Europeans anyhow, so why so much fuss about a little massacre at My Lai?

I wonder how many of us are conscious that nothing but racial prejudice of the worst kind is at the base of such complaisance. Would those pro-Vietnam War Americans hold their views so firmly if such daily body counts and graphic pictures of suffering came from Europe or if the Vietnamese were white? I think not. And a little American-born Japanese boy in Chicago did not think so either. His father was a respected professor at the University of Chicago, where he daily watched the body count and other military activities in Vietnam on television. Today he and his parents are no longer in Chicago. They reluctantly decided to return to Japan after the father could not deal with this persistent question from the little boy: "*Otosan* (father), why are they so cruel to people like us?"

The fact is that many Americans maintain two yardsticks of humanity, freedom, and decency: a superior one applicable to themselves and other Whites, and an inferior one applicable to the rest of the world, including Asians. This was why Japanese citizens, residents and aliens alike, were put in concentration camps during World War II while German Americans were unrestrained despite the fact that Germany was the chief architect of both world wars. To justify this double standard, Americans need to maintain their erroneous notions about Asians, thereby enabling themselves to live with the sharp conflicts between their belief in Christian love, democracy, freedom, and equality on the one hand and their blatant disregard for these values in action on the other hand. However, the most pernicious myths about Asians and other minority groups are those cloaked in pseudoscientific respectability. They are, therefore, hidden prejudices, and are much more pervasive and much more difficult to eradicate than restrictions which force non-Whites to less desirable housing and blind-alley occupations.

The Myth of Chinese Expansionism

One such pernicious American prejudice against China since the Communist Revolution of 1949 is the myth of Chinese expansionism. We already noted one important argument contrary to this belief, namely the centripetal or inward-looking tendency of the Chinese as expressed in their lack of desire to emigrate (Chapter 5). Now we shall examine the question from other angles.

Since 1949, those who profess to fear Chinese expansionism have persistently pointed to China's actions vis-à-vis Tibet and India: (a) the 1950 military occupation of Tibet, (b) the 1962 attack on India, and (c) the building of a road through Ladakh linking Sinkiang with Tibet. However, none of these is a good indication of expansionism; they are either measures to redress past grievances or to secure immediate borders. They involve no stakes far away from China's home base, and no *new* territorial and political goals. Furthermore, on at least the first two items the Nationalist and Communist governments are in complete accord.

A little history will help put China's occupation of Tibet into perspective. The region had long been under Chinese suzerainty. But since the 1850's, when China was militarily prostrate, both the British and the Russians vied for control as part of their world-wide expansionist drives. Among the first acts of such expansionists were efforts to "divide and conquer"—to bribe or coerce local leaders into declaring independence or concluding a bilateral treaty, without China, as a prelude to annexation by the expansionist powers. Thus Japan made the Korean king declare independence in 1895 before annexing Korea in 1910; Japan created "Manchukuo" and imported the puppet emperor P'u Yi after Manchuria was conquered in 1931. Various European aggressors signed agreements with regional Chinese warlords during 1911–1928 to create the so-called Spheres of Influence which constituted de facto dissection of the country. China's move into Tibet in 1950 was part of an effort to regain control she had had earlier.

A comparison between the Chinese link with Tibet and that which exists between the United States and Hawaii or Alaska may seem fantastic to some readers, but it is nevertheless both reasonable and sound. Chinese suzerainty over Tibet has a much longer history than that of the United States over Hawaii or Alaska. Would the United States react kindly to any bilateral agreement between any of the Hawaiian kings or their descendants which might repudiate American control over the Islands? The United States bought Alaska from Russia; neither party to the transaction consulted the Eskimos. Would the United States not flex her military muscles if the Eskimos now decided to go to the United Nations or otherwise gain independence? Among the family of nations, no less than in domestic affairs within any one society, the same logic and yardstick must apply to all cases if peace is truly desired; it is the height of folly to use double standards.

The Chinese–Indian border dispute was of British origin. Following her military expedition to Lhasa under Younghusband in 1904, Britain, as ruler over India, laid down the law to the Chinese and the Tibetans at the Simla Convention of 1913. The British drew up the McMahon Line in a treaty which the Chinese government, even though no military match for the British at the time, never ratified. From 1950 on, the Chinese and Indian governments entered into almost continuous negotiations on the border question. Those who care to examine the facts will find that it was after the Indians forcibly occupied the disputed territories that the Chinese decided to "teach the Indians a lesson."

Furthermore, and this is a most important point, the Chinese stopped their advance as soon as they restored the border condition to status quo ante. Had China been bent on expansionism, she could easily have fished in the troubled waters of Northeast Assam, where the people have more racial affinity with the Chinese than with the Indians and where Naga rebellion and demand for independence have long been festering. Following the well-beaten path of expansionist powers, China could have sent in "advisors," trained Naga guerrillas, supplied the Nagas with military aid, and even signed a bilateral treaty with Naga leaders treating Nagaland as an "independent" state. But China did none of these.

Even the Chinese road through Ladakh is not without some legal foundation. The world knows about the military clashes between India and Pakistan over Jammu and Kashmir; the status of the region is in dispute despite Indian occupation of most of it. *A Map Folio of Communist China* dated October 1967, produced by the C.I.A., uses "status in dispute" to describe that region. It separates Jammu and Kashmir on the one hand and China on the other *not with the usual symbols of international boundaries but with those for unsettled ones.*

In view of the fact that China and Pakistan have already signed treaties concerning their mutual boundaries, is it not possible that the former has obtained the latter's permission (as party to the territory she considers her own) to build that road?

Chinese Pattern with Tributary States

Having an inward-looking orientation before the twentieth century, China had never actively sought contact with non-Chinese states as long as her security was not threatened. This pattern has two facets. On the one hand, the Chinese have no history of proselytization and crusades to crush or "save" the "infidels," a fact we noted in Chapter 6. The non-Chinese peoples, including Koreans, Japanese, Vietnamese, and Siamese (Thais) who voluntarily sent representatives and students to China were met with all sorts of "Unwelcome" signs when they arrived in China.[1] In spite of this, the non-Chinese peoples continued to come and assiduously imported Chinese art, poetry, literature, ancestor worship and Buddhism, institutions, ethics and philosophy, craftsmanship, written language and literary concepts, building and clothing styles, and even manners.

On the other hand, the Chinese way of dealing with what she self-importantly called the "barbarians" was centered in the notion of *p'ing* or pacification. Except for a few rulers, such as Emperor Wu (140–87 B.C.) of the Han dynasty, whom Chinese historians later derogatorily characterized as *hao ta hsi kung* (likes bigness and loves military conquests), the Chinese hope was usually for the maintenance of status quo rather than for expansionism.

To secure that end, the Chinese emperors often followed the capitalistic rule of minimum effort for maximum result. For example, in 618 A.D., the Tibetan King Songtsen Gampo sought the hand in marriage of a daughter of the T'ang emperor. To impress the Chinese with the seriousness of his request, the Tibetan king amassed an army of 200,000 troops and occupied Chinese territory in the province of Szechuan. Of course, his request was granted. But that did not settle things for long. Another Tibetan ruler, after marrying a Chinese princess under similar circumstances, asked for various Chinese classics and histories. In 730 A.D., when this request had been refused twice, and his Chinese queen had died, he invaded China with a 400,000 man force. In 763 A.D., Tibet reached her acme. King Trisong Detsen's 200,000 man force went as far as Ch'ang An—then the national capital—and sacked it. The reigning T'ang emperor fled and the Tibetans installed a puppet Chinese emperor on whom they forced a treaty of submission and annual tribute in Chinese fashion; the arrangement did not, however, endure.

In spite of such occasional setbacks, the prestige of China and the Chinese civilization continued to be high, for quite a few non-Chinese states *chose* to be related to the Chinese court by way of the tribute system. Most Westerners, scholars and others alike, have confused the Chinese tribute system, which does not accord with their psychology, with the Western colonial system, which they understand only too well. The Chinese tribute system involved, principally, acknowledgement of tributary status on the part of a non-Chinese government to the Chinese court, and the dispatch of gift-bearing envoys to the Chinese capital at regular intervals, but this involved no Chinese control of its internal and external affairs, and no colonization by Chinese people.[2]

However, the tribute system was not necessarily good business for the Chinese even when they were most often the superior party to it. To begin with, the envoys and their entourages had to be properly and ceremonially taken care of by the local authorities as soon as they reached Chinese soil. For those from the South Seas this meant all the way from Kwangtung province in the extreme South to Peking in the far North. The speediest transit for the envoys and the extensive and bulky gifts they bore, which often included pairs of male and female elephants and other live animals, would require six months or more. Furthermore, the Chinese emperors not only had to entertain the envoys and their entourages lavishly at the court but, being in the superior's position, had to reciprocate with gifts often more expensive than the ones received.

Consequently, in the Ming dynasty (1368–1644 A.D.), one Chinese emperor asked the king of Siam (now Thailand), in whose domain Chinese soldiers never set foot, *not to send any more tribute delegations,* at least for awhile. Even then, the Siamese rulers did not oblige by stopping their tributary missions. In this context, we can understand why each ruler of Siam, Japan, and Okinawa at one time or another requested the Chinese court to confer upon him an Imperial Seal of Office for sanctification of his rule.

Communist China's Deeds

Finally the expansionism attributed to China must be seen in light of her Communist government's performance. Before the rise of that government, Western opinion about China and the Chinese was a different matter entirely. In fact, between World Wars I and II, China was an object of international pity and sympathy. Some Westerners kept their admiration for Chinese philosophies, manners, and objets d'art while others sent charity from time to time or worked for China's salvation through conversion to Christianity or industrialization. But many saw her poverty and famine, warlordism, official corruption, and military weakness with exasperation and disgust. No one at that time would term the Chinese and their government expansionist. The latter view came only after 1949. What, then, are the Chinese actions under the present government which have fed the myth of Chinese expansionism?

The answer is that objective facts in support of that belief are lacking. The People's Republic of China was and is certainly belligerent in words. Some of her leaders have openly spoken of "wars of liberation" among non-Chinese nations as necessary steps to world socialism. But how readily and frequently has the Chinese government sent its armed forces abroad?

If we use the criterion of words to judge Chinese intentions we must do the same with the United States. In 1950 no less a person than former U.S. Secretary of the Navy, Daniel Kimball, said of the scientist, Ch'ien Hsueh-shen, who wanted to leave the United States for mainland China:

I'd rather shoot that guy than let him out of the country. He knows too much that is valuable to us. He's worth five divisions anywhere.[3]

But the United States, after persecuting and detaining Ch'ien for five years, did not commit the atrocity of shooting the man and did allow him to leave. Then, since 1949, there have been American plans to invade China and many Americans in high places have openly talked about it, but no such invasion has taken place.

The fact is, every nation, like every individual, entertains thoughts or makes utterances which are never acted upon because of inability, force of circumstances, or *because the words are intended to substitute for actions in the first place.* Politicians and diplomats act in that manner all too frequently everywhere.

The record shows that China has been extremely prudent in military involvements abroad. The Chinese did not enter the Korean War until General MacArthur's forces were close to the Yalu River and the General threatened to cross it.[4] Once the truce was signed, the Chinese forces left North Korea while a sizable contingent of American forces remained in South Korea. The Chinese have yet to become a belligerent in the Vietnam War. There has been no military response in spite of heavy American bombing close to the Chinese borders and constant American reconnaissance flights over Chinese territory.

There is, then, a curious contrast. The Chinese leaders say they want to liberate the world, but they make few or no military excursions abroad. Our leaders say they have no territorial ambitions and wish nothing but peace, freedom, and happiness for all peoples, but we have permanent and semi-permanent armed bases everywhere and systematically destroy all recalcitrant Asians who refuse to acknowledge American supremacy and knuckle down under American might. In this process many innocent Asian civilians are, of course, butchered, but many Americans simply say, "That's war!"

An American Psychological Need

If the facts are so blatantly contrary to the myth of Chinese expansionism, why do so many Americans insist that China is expansionist? I think the answer is quite clear.

First, mainland China is under a Communist government and Americans still deeply fear Communism.[5] Since Communism as an ideology is expansionist, it is believed that China under Communism is bound to be expansionist according to this Aristotelian syllogism. Under the circumstances, the fact of China's long historical trend of centripetalism is denied. Americans are not aware that the Chinese, even when they have become Christians, have no zeal for expansionist proselytization.

Second, China is Asian and non-White, and has the largest population in the world. As a weak and helpless Asian nation of immense size, China was a nuisance but tolerable. Now that she has become a self-reliant, defiant giant, freed from famine and regional warlords, and Communist to boot, the situation is just too overwhelming for those Americans consciously or unconsciously steeped in the notion of American or white supremacy.[6]

Third, belief in and fear of Chinese expansionism is a psychological necessity for a historically and still expansionist West. This necessity has two aspects. Those who are prone to expansionism must fear expansionism by their victims. This is why many Whites fear improvement of Blacks—they know what they themselves would do to their former oppressors once the tables were turned. The other aspect is that expansionist powers need to create expansionist enemies to justify their own expansionist acts and designs.[7]

The Stake of the Chinese in America

This somewhat extended analysis of the false foundation on which the notion of Chinese expansionism was built may seem out of place in a book on the Chinese in America. It is not. Like a spider's web, a people's behavior—infinitely complex and varied though it may appear on the surface—has a common thread which links all of its ramifications.

The belief in Chinese expansionism and the related Domino Theory are the foundation of the Vietnam War. The validity of the Domino Theory has sometimes been disputed, but the false notion of Chinese expansionism is cited again and again as justification for American intervention in Vietnam and for all the American casualties and Vietnamese suffering. President Nixon specifically did so as recently as his July 1, 1970, television interview.

The Chinese in America, by virtue of their Chinese racial and cultural origin and their American citizenship, cannot be separated from a matter of such grave moment. By the tie of citizenship they have to pay for and send their sons to fight in the war in Vietnam or elsewhere. By the tie of origin they will always be seen by the white American public as having something to do with China and her real or imagined behavior. In a society where public image opens and closes a lot of doors, this is especially important. The public image of the Chinese in America has suffered by vicious white prejudices which propel their holders to generate more falsehoods about China and the Chinese.[8]

It is no accident that in two decades of intensive search for a policy toward mainland China, few Americans of Chinese descent have ever been called to testify in Congress about China. An immigrant German–American, Henry Kissinger, now sits in President Nixon's innermost council of advisors, but no Chinese–American even heads any of the committees dealing with China in any of the powerful foundations granting millions of dollars for research on China.

The matter does not stop at the level of public image and opportunities for advancement. The Chinese in America must reflect on the fate of the Jews in Nazi Germany and the Japanese in America after Pearl Harbor. Many of the German Jews had been bred in the country for countless generations and were thoroughly German in language, taste, and manners. Furthermore, most of them were not physically distinguishable from other Germans, and many were not even believers in the Jewish faith. But in the end it was a false belief in their so-called "common conspiracy against Germany and the German people," (by then they were not called Germans), that publicly justified subjecting those German Jews to inhuman treatment including mass execution in crematoria.

White America dealt with the Japanese better than Nazi Germany did with the Jews. But the brutal treatment of the Japanese–Americans—concentration camps euphemistically called relocation centers—was not something white America would have tolerated or endorsed had the Japanese been white. That harsh white American treatment of Japanese–Americans was also based on a false belief: the treacherousness of all Japanese, which endangered American security. And that belief was not founded on what the Japanese in America had or had not done, but on what the Japanese government and the Japanese in Japan had perpetrated.

In the end, not one Japanese–American was convicted or even implicated as a spy for Japan. On the contrary, the proof of their patriotism to the United States on the battlefield and in every other way was astonishing. But no amount of disclaimer by individual Jews in Nazi Germany and by individual Japanese in California during World War II saved them from their common fate as Jews or Japanese.

Unless the Chinese in America understand the implications of the present false belief about Chinese expansionism and do something to remove or at least mitigate it instead of letting it grow as events drift, their day of rude awakening may not be far off. For dark clouds in the latter direction are already gathering in high places. J. Edgar Hoover, in testifying before a subcommittee of the House Committee on Appropriations on April 17, 1969, said, "the blatant, belligerent, and illogical statements made by Red China's spokesmen during the past year leave no doubt that the United States is Communist China's No. 1 enemy." He then went on to warn the subcommittee of Communist Chinese intelligence activity "overt and covert, to obtain needed material, particularly in the scientific field."

And then Mr. Hoover became specific. After hinting darkly that a Chinese–American sentenced to 60 days in jail for making a false customs declaration about electronic parts being sent to Hong Kong might have been a Communist agent, he continued:

We are being confronted with a growing amount of work in being alert for Chinese–Americans and others in this country who would assist Red China in supplying needed material or promoting Red Chinese propaganda....

For one thing, Red China has been flooding the country with its propaganda and there are over 300,000 Chinese in the United States, some of whom could be susceptible to recruitment either through ethnic ties or hostage situations because of relatives in Communist China.... Up to 20,000 Chinese immigrants can come into the United States each year, and this provides a means to send illegal agents into our nation.... There are active Chinese Communist sympathizers in the Western Hemisphere in a position to aid in operations against the United States.

The sociologist Stanford M. Lyman, commenting on the Hoover testimony, observed:

Thus the Chinese in America were reminded that perhaps all their efforts at convincing white America that they were a peaceable, law-abiding, family-minded, and docile people who contributed much and asked little in return had gone for naught. In time of crisis they, too, might suffer the same fate that overtook the highly acculturated Japanese–Americans a quarter century before—wholesale incarceration.[9]

It is clear that our comparison of the situation of the Chinese–Americans today with those of Jews before the rise of Nazism in Germany and of Japanese–Americans during World War II is not illogical or fantastic. Quite the contrary. When a false belief is needed to persecute a whole people in racial terms, no member of that group is exempt. In this the Western way of exclusiveness in affiliation and absolutism in religion can only add oil to the fire. The Chinese–Americans must see that, even more important than individual advancements through better jobs and housing, they have no alternative but to actively work toward eliminating on the one hand, false and malicious beliefs about China and the Chinese in general, and on the other hand, the possibility of a military confrontation between their country of origin and their country of birth or adoption.

The Roots of Prejudice

In working to reduce or eliminate prejudice we are often trapped in an erroneous assumption, that prejudice is caused only by individuals who are prejudiced. On that basis, the Chinese in America would be able to reduce or stop the danger of Hooverism against Chinese–Americans if they could make Hoover retract his maligning testimony or force Hoover out of office. Nothing is further from the truth. They should realize that President Roosevelt could not have ordered the incarceration of the West Coast Japanese in World War II if a majority or even a sizable minority of white Americans were truly opposed to it. That opposition was sadly lacking. In the long run people get the kind of government and leaders they deserve. In fact, in our kind of society that statement is more true than in many of its less democratic counterparts. That Mr. Hoover is able to survive political changes and hold on to his power for so long must be regarded as prima facie evidence that his attitude and action patterns are in tune with those of a majority of Whites. Consequently, even if Mr. Hoover is dismissed, the chances are that someone like him will fill his shoes.

In a similar light, we must see a different kind of questionable behavior toward the Chinese by another public official—in this case, Secretary of Transportation Volpe. On May 10, 1869, the Union Pacific Railroad coming from Omaha and the Central Pacific Railroad coming from Sacramento joined each other at Promontory, Utah, near Ogden. The magnificent role of the Chinese workers in this historical accomplishment, which we brie. y mentioned in Chapter 1, is now public knowledge. But the Chinese workers were not allowed to be part of the celebration which ensued. The white workers (many of them Irish) and the officials physically prevented Chinese from being present on this occasion.

One hundred years later, on May 10, 1969, the centennial of the event was celebrated. As its chief speaker, Secretary Volpe deliberately omitted any reference to the Chinese contribution in his glowing tribute to the American people. Protests by some West Coast Chinese organizations followed, but I have not seen any corrective remarks by Volpe's office. Thus, although 100 years have elapsed, the same racial prejudice has persisted. One could argue that perhaps a less prejudiced Secretary of Transportation would have given the Chinese railroad workers more justice. But once again, we must remember that as a high government official, Volpe did not speak for himself, alone. His speech must have been prepared by his many staff members, and it was intended for national consumption.

The roots of prejudice are in the interpersonal situation, not the individual. Of course, individuals vary in disposition, character, and vested interest. But no individual can stand alone. He must cooperate and deal with the pressure or threat or esteem of his fellow human beings in his neighborhood, club, school, factory, party, circle of friends, or community. It is here that what seems an individual matter is really a group affair.

Since, in our individualist society, each man is enjoined to be self-reliant, no one has a permanent place in the social scheme of things. All statuses are subject to change without notice. While each individual is always anxious to look above for possible steps to climb, he is at the same time continuously threatened by possible encroachment from below. In his ceaseless effort at achieving and maintaining status, he fears being "contaminated" by those deemed inferior, and he cherishes and seeks symbols or privileges associated with those he considers equal or superior.

In this process, it is obvious that not all persons can be on top, or even at a station which they can consider satisfactory. Consequently, while the fortunate ones who achieve success, superiority, and triumph may bask in the sunshine, they must do so on the basis of failure, inferiority, and defeat on the part of the less fortunate. For the latter, and for a majority who fear they may not make it in the end, the resentment against and fear of failure, inferiority, and defeat must be widespread and often unbearable. They must find ways of assuring themselves that they are not failures, inferiors, and the vanquished. Acts of prejudice toward some minority group at least provide them with an illusion of success, superiority, and triumph.

Since individuals vary in the extent to which they are pressed by this fear of inferiority, they act differently. Some will join hate organizations, lynching mobs, and throw stones at homes of Blacks or paint swastikas on Jewish synagogues. These are violent acts of prejudice. Others will do everything they legally (or secretly and deviously) can to keep individuals or minority religious, racial, or ethnic groups out of residential areas, occupational opportunities, and social fraternities. These are active nonviolent acts of prejudice. Still others will quietly refuse to associate with members of such minorities and teach their children to observe this taboo because "one just does not do such things." These are passive nonviolent acts of prejudice.

However he translates his fear of inferiority into action, many—perhaps most—self-reliant white Americans find it difficult to act in accordance with the much repeated American values of equality or the Christian life. It is not that they desire contradiction or are, as their critics often charge, hypocritical. It is simply that they are oppressed by fears of losing status—fears deeply rooted in a relatively free society where no human network is permanent. This is where personal and seemingly trivial acts of prejudice and discrimination on a national scale meet. The former are the foundation of the latter. This is why, though many Southern Whites are not personally against Blacks, they nevertheless do not dare to run the risk of being branded "Nigger lovers."

There is, however, an optimistic note to this otherwise depressing analysis of prejudice in America. There are some who, in their zeal against racism, tend to group the United States together with the Union of South Africa, where the doctrine of White Supremacy prevails. But a real gulf separates the two nations. In the Union of South Africa, racism exists in daily life and as a matter of public policy. Over the last two decades, this government has greatly escalated and sharpened whatever racism had previously governed the life of the people; it is actively engaged in strengthening racism in education, trade, residential patterns, religion, justice, and occupational opportunities—all designed to keep the Blacks down in perpetuity.

In the United States, on the other hand, most of the overall legal developments and educational policies during the last two decades have aimed at eradicating racism and redressing its cumulative historical effects. There are still strong regional differences and resistances, but these are generally so-called defensive measures. Except for those who have to use racism as an instrument for power, such as George Wallace of Alabama, most politicians and public administrators, even if they do not personally care for racial equality, have to disclaim, directly or indirectly, their racist intentions.

Governments and leaders can influence the general public and get the ball rolling in the desired direction just as the psychological pressures and fears on the part of the man on the street cannot help but guide or motivate those in high places in the long run. There is no doubt that the social and political fabric of the American society is moving toward greater egalitarianism every day and in ever widening circles.[10] When the Pilgrims first settled here it was equality among white Protestants only. Soon that equality was extended to include all Christians, then the Jews, and now the Blacks and the Orientals. A group of American Indians has just occupied Alcatraz Island near San Francisco. That symbolic act signifies that the most deprived and the least articulate original Americans have finally awakened to their need for an equal share of the American dream.

I wonder, though, if American aggressiveness in Asia, and the contempt with which white American soldiers reportedly hold the average Vietnamese whom they have gone out to help or liberate, are not in some unconscious way related to the gradual loss of elbow room for inequality at home. Individuals who have the psychological need for constant reassurance of their superiority must find other individuals on whom they can exercise that superiority. That helps explain why so many Americans still insist on seeing China as the expansionist villain that she in fact is not.

I wonder. But I hope not.

Notes

1. The reader interested in knowing more about this can consult the work of a Japanese monk entitled *Ennin's Diary: The Record of a Pilgrimage to China in Search of the Law* (New York: Ronald Press, 1955), translated and annotated by Edwin O. Reischauer, Professor of Japanese History at Harvard University and former American Ambassador to Japan.

2. One Western scholar who understands this is John K. Fairbank. (See "China's Foreign Policy in Historical Perspective," *Foreign Affairs,* April 1969, pp. 449–463.) He also points out that some states entered the tributary system voluntarily because of the profit motive.

3. *Honolulu Advertiser,* April 27, 1970.

4. Those Americans who refuse to see Chinese incursion in Korea as an inevitable defensive maneuver need only reflect on how they would feel if Chinese forces were operating in Mexico and their commander-in-chief threatened to cross the Rio Grande. Would they support a policy of non-intervention? We have already discussed the absurdity and untenability of international double standards.

5. In a recent article, Robert L. Heilbroner asks the intriguing question, is the U.S. fundamentally opposed to economic development? ("The Revolution of Rising Expectations: Rhetoric and Reality," in N. D. Houghton, ed., *Struggle against History: U.S. Foreign Policy in an Age of Revolution* [New York: Clarion, 1968], p. 106). This question, which must seem fantastic to some readers, cannot be easily dismissed. The Cambridge economist Joan Robinson answers it in the affirmative: "It is obvious enough that the United States' crusade against Communism is a campaign against development." ("Contrasts in Economic Development: China and India," in N. D. Houghton, ed., *ibid.,* p. 134.) We may not be able to endorse Dr. Robinson's view completely, but the weight of her logic is considerable. Dr. Hiroshi Kitamura, Senior Specialist at the East–West Center and formerly Director of Research and Planning, Economic Commission for Asia and the Far East (ECAFE), United Nations' ECAFE Secretariat, Bangkok, Thailand, explains the question by noting the basically revolutionary nature of the development process. "Development is much more than a matter of increasing national product within a given social structure; it is, rather, a process of ideational, social, economic, and political change that affects the basic structure of society. If the struggle of ideologies is used to suppress popular movements aiming at such changes everywhere in the world, there is an obvious danger that the well-intentioned containment policy may degenerate into a simple maneuver to maintain status quo. From an economist's viewpoint, this is the basic weakness of the Cold War strategy, as it has been applied against China in Asia." ("Asia's Future in Asian Perspective," paper read at a Conference on "After Vietnam, What?", May 22, 1970, on the occasion of the Inauguration of Dr. Harlan Cleveland as President of the University of Hawaii.

6. Why Americans so deeply fear Communism has interesting psychological implications. See Francis L. K. Hsu, "World Unrest, Communism, and America," *Americans and Chinese: Purpose and Fulfillment in Great Civilizations* (New York: Natural History Press, 1970), Chapter 16.

7. Another interesting question is why some present-day governments in Southeast Asia also believe in, or profess the fear of, Chinese "expansionism." This is analyzed in Francis L. K. Hsu, "The Myth of Chinese Expansionism," (to be published).

8. Some of my critics do not entirely agree with my position here. Dr. Donald Char, Professor of Public Health at the University of Hawaii, thinks that my statements of white prejudice are too strong. "I do not personally believe that there is that much malice or deep-seated feeling toward us as yellow men." However, Char continues, "but I would agree that there exists a subconscious belittling or condescension on the part of many white Americans towards us, making it very difficult for us to react effectively with them at times." (Personal communication). Mrs. John Israel, who holds a B.A. from Stanford University and an M.A. from Radcliffe College, and is the wife of a professor at the University of Virginia, says she, too, feels my "statements of white prejudice are far too strong. I have personally run into more prejudice as a woman than as a Chinese–American." She continues, "I do not believe that most Americans look upon Chinese–Americans as linked with Communist China any more than they regard Russo–Americans as Bolsheviks" (personal communication).

9. Stanford M. Lyman, "Red Guard on Grant Avenue," *Trans*-action, Vol. 7, No. 6, April 1970 (Special Issue), p. 34. Some Chinese–Americans have fought sporadically

against such forces of oppression. On March 2, 1956, the United States Attorney-General's office in San Francisco convened a Grand Jury and subpoenaed all the records of most district and family associations. The presence of Chinese Communists among immigrants was cited as a principal cause for this action. The Chinese community labeled this action as racist, retained legal counsel, and successfully prevented the records from being used. The Grand Jury found none of the allegations true. I am indebted to Professor Kenneth A. Abbott for this information.

10. Support for this observation is also found in a recent article entitled "Orientals Find Bias Is Down Sharply in U.S." in the *New York Times* (December 13, 1970). For this reason I do not entirely agree with Dr. Lyman's observation that the same fate as the Japanese–American suffered in World War II may await the Chinese–American if war were to break out between China and the United States. Mrs. John Israel, whose comments we noted before, reminds me of the fact that "there was no ... reaction" against American–Chinese "during the Korean conflict when Chinese troops were fighting Americans. Chinese–Americans were intelligence officers and interpreters in the field, quite unlike the Japanese–Americans who were sent to the European theater during World War II, either because they were not to be trusted to fight other Japanese, or perhaps might be mistaken for the enemy." (Personal communication.) Times are different, world opinion has changed somewhat, and America has evolved.

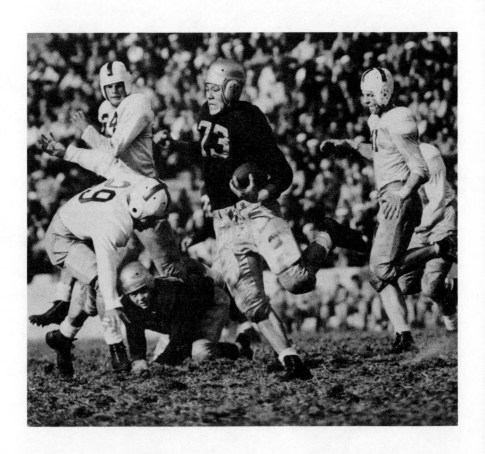

George Fong, right halfback for the University of California, about to score.
(Photograph courtesy of Brown Brothers.)

Chapter Ten

Americanization and the American Dream

Among the Chinese in America, as among other immigrant or minority groups, one often hears, by way of explaining or excusing some individual's behavior, "He is entirely Americanized." I have encountered Chinese parents who express themselves in this vein about their children, students about themselves or each other, and wives about their husbands. I have even had white colleagues tell me they liked me because I was "so American." And at an annual convention of the American Anthropological Association, a fellow anthropologist characterized me privately as being "very Americanized, very aggressive," all in the same breath.

Within that large bag of the term "Americanization" are subsumed diverse meanings: naiveté about Chinese customs, lack of facility in Chinese language, success and bigger success, initiative, dignity of labor, frankness in approach, selfish and egotistical attitudes, suaveness in dealing with policemen when caught violating traffic rules, ingenuity, perfect command of English, aggressiveness, optimism, love of gadgetry, flamboyance, business before sentiment, expressing one's own views without hesitation, "running around the house as one likes," "dating whomever one pleases," devotion to church and its activities, and thinking big. The list by no means exhausts all meanings I have come across, but it is an average and reasonable sample.

It seems clear that we do not have a precise idea as to what we mean by "Americanization," nor have anthropologists who deal with culture contact and culture change helped in this regard. For example, they use the term "acculturation" to describe changes in the life style of various American

Indian tribes. But what they have done is to note certain modifications of the Indians' tribal cultures without drawing up any systematic and comprehensive picture of the American culture to which the Indians are acculturating themselves. How can we gauge the extent of acculturation without precise notions about the culture to which the acculturated have supposedly acculturated themselves?

The Meaning of Americanization

What do we mean when we say of an immigrant, "He is Americanized?" From the sample list just given and from our experiences, we cannot but agree that the picture is by no means clear. We must develop a more precise idea on the notion of Americanization to answer the question at all.

As I see it, two basic parts are involved in the definition of this term. The first is a functioning membership in the American society. The second is the assumption of attitudes and behavior patterns compatible with being a member of the American society, whether in discharging one's duties or in enjoying one's privileges.

The first part is relatively simple. It includes citizenship but also the following elements:

1. Occupational competence for economic independence;
2. Clothing, residential pattern, and style of life acceptable to a majority of other Americans;
3. Minimal command of the English language adequate for occupational and social purposes;
4. A certain amount of participation in community affairs;
5. Voting and reasonable participation in political activity on behalf of oneself or others;
6. Ability to resort to law for self-protection and for furtherance of one's interests.[1]

The second part, namely attitudes and behavior patterns compatible with being a member of the American society, is much more complex but nevertheless may be stated with more or less clarity. Elsewhere I have analyzed the American and Chinese ways of life in terms of postulates which are "broadly generalized propositions" held by members of every ongoing society "as to the nature of things and as to what is qualitatively desirable and undesirable." [2] Without encumbering ourselves with all the details, I shall present below seven simplified postulates which, in my view, govern the attitudes and behavior patterns of a majority of Americans.

1. The most important concern of every individual is self-interest, self-expression, self-development, self-gratification, autonomy, and independence. This self-in-

terest takes precedence over group interest except in an extreme emergency. This proposition expresses itself in a wide range of ways, from independence of children, the notion that altruism is suspect, the search for identity, all the way to severe competitiveness, emphasis on individual privacy, ambition, and creativity.

2. Government exists for the benefit of the individual and not vice versa. All forms of authority, including that of government, are suspect, but the government and its symbols should be respected. Patriotism is good. This proposition embraces a basic contradiction and therefore expresses itself in conflicting ways. On the one hand, people must watch the government and participate in the political process; on the other hand, there is resentment against dissent.

3. An individual's success in life depends upon his acceptance among his peers. This means combining with others to further his self-interest, but not becoming so deeply involved with them that vertical or horizontal mobility are impossible. Nothing succeeds like success.

4. An individual should believe in or acknowledge God and should belong to an organized church or other religious institution. Religion is good. Any religion is better than no religion. Hence individuals who do not belong to churches are socially abnormal, and those who deny the existence of God or who think churches are bad are suspect. There is only one God.[3]

5. Men and women are equal, as are all human beings. The obvious inequalities at any given point of time due to race, class, national origin, religion, and education, are temporary. Education will eradicate some of them. Individual initiative will do the rest. Only innate differences (such as intelligence or disposition) can justify permanent inequalities.

6. Progress is good and inevitable. An individual must improve himself by minimizing his efforts and maximizing his returns, and the government must be more efficient to tackle new problems. Institutions such as churches must modernize themselves to be more attractive. Education and wealth are absolute goods and are the two chief means for all kinds of progress. Progress means that the young know better than the old. Progress means that good will drive out evil, as the two cannot coexist.

7. Being American is synonymous with being progressive, and America is the utmost symbol of progress. Therefore, the United States has a mission to spread Americanism to all peoples of the world. Obstructions to this diffusion are intolerable and must be eliminated or destroyed (by war if necessary) until American good prevails, and those who seek American help and guidance and acknowledge the superiority of Americans and Americanism are given American charity and know-how so that they will become Americanized.

It is clear that some of these postulates differ greatly from some American ideals. "Love thy neighbor" and "turn the other cheek" are still a part of American ideals (certainly I have not seen any open repudiation of them), but they are not operating postulates. Some of the postulates are inconsistent with others. Equality of all mankind is incommensurate with the notion of American superiority over all others. However, human beings rarely worry about the inconsistencies between one postulate and another, or between ideal and reality, since they normally do not assess their actions in overall terms. Instead they gloss over the inconsistencies or add riders such as "you have to be realistic" to tide over whatever mental discomfort they may experience at particular times and in particular contexts.

Creative Adjustment

If we look at these postulates closely we can classify them into two broad groups. The first group has four component ideas: (a) individual independence, (b) individual success based on competition, initiative, and creativity, (c) active participation in the political process, and (d) zeal for idealism which embodies cause-orientation and the right and duty to dissent. These are the attitudes which have made the United States of America a Great Society and the envy of the rest of the world.

On the other hand, the second group centers around four other components which are not so salutary: (a) American supremacy, (b) prejudice based on race, religion, or national origin, (c) unmitigated self-interest which leads to accelerated criminality, environmental pollution, and alienation, and (d) corruption at public expense and decimation of family and kinship relationships, which in turn serve to foster juvenile delinquency and rootlessness in general. These are ideational forces which gnaw at the foundation of American society and threaten its very existence.[4]

Immigrants and native-born American minorities have generally two alternative ways of approaching Americanization. They can simply try their best to assume the attitudes and action patterns of the majority Whites without selection—"when in Rome do as the Romans do." And, like teenagers, the fear of rejection by the majority may even goad them into more exaggerated attitudes and action patterns so that they appear at least superficially more American than native white Americans.

On the other hand, they can make some evaluation of the merits or demerits of the attitudes and action patterns prevalent among white Americans and consciously direct themselves toward and prepare their children for a degree of selectiveness in the process of their Americanization. In this they will not follow the line of least resistance. In fact, this is a much rockier road, for not only is it harder to travel, but also some voyagers are likely to meet with rejection and hostility and even be branded un-American. More than once I have seen an indignant white American throw the following question at an immigrant American speaker who criticized some aspect of American life or policy: "If you don't like America, why did you come here?" There are even Americans who have publicly voiced the view that native-born white dissenters should all be shipped to Russia.

The reader who has come this far will surely be able to see how the Chinese in America *can* take the line of least resistance on their way to Americanization. With industry, high value for education, and a desire for advancement bred in their Chinese cultural roots, they can simply look for avenues of success open to them: make money through business; enter legal, medical, and dental professions and build up lucrative practices; or join administrative services and become trusted bureaucrats who will act only in accordance with predetermined rules. Some of these become tycoons; they will thus have achieved success as Americans.[5]

In this respect, the transition to American ways is relatively easy for many Chinese. In fact, many Chinese attitudes and behavior characteristics are facilitated and rewarded within the American context.

For example, the Chinese pattern of mutual help among family members and relatives and fellow-locals dovetails well with the American pattern of individual independence. From the point of view of the Whites, the Chinese have rarely been in need of public assistance. This pattern has in the past tended to be a factor for keeping many Chinese among the Chinese. Yet the American context eliminates many traditional Chinese drawbacks. For one thing, being away from China, the number of relatives even for large families is smaller than what it would have been in the old country. The American context also makes it possible for more Chinese to deal with business transactions before or without considering nonbusiness ties. Although they do not always do so, they can always use the rules and regulations inherent in the American situation to excuse themselves should nonbusiness demands conflict with their business interests. General Ts'ai T'ing-kai, famed for his defense of Shanghai against the Japanese in 1932, whom we met in Chapter 1, tells in his autobiography how, before deciding to join the army, his little store located in a small town of Kwangtung province went bankrupt because of the unreasonable demands of his relatives and local people.[6] His countrymen in America do not have to suffer from such disabilities.

A different kind of transition concerns nepotism and bureaucratic corruption in general. Nepotism, that is, favoritism in awarding public appointments to one's relatives, was well known in China before 1949. It also extended to those with local ties. The American kinship pattern, because of the individual's need to reject or replace parental ties with other links, is an insurance against nepotism as practiced in traditional China. The American pattern, however, favors a new kind of nepotism and official corruption on a grander scale.

One form this American nepotism takes is not totally dissimilar to its Chinese counterpart. Legislators in Washington, D.C., usually try to get federal appointments for faithfuls of their constituencies, thereby diverting federal money in the form of aid and projects into their own state. But two much more widespread American practices are (a) the cultivation and favoring of useful cronies regardless of kinship and locality and (b) influence peddling and buying. The object of the latter is not embezzlement (as was common in traditional China) but the gathering of government plums for one's preserves in diverse lines of endeavors. Plying officials with luxurious hospitality and gifts of vicuña coats or stocks so that they will favor their benefactors with giant government contracts is one object. Getting the officials to grant development rights and mineral concessions, which may lead to far greater returns over longer periods of time, is another.[7]

The Chinese understand this very well and, once in a position to do so, need very little cultural transition to become Americanized in this respect. Furthermore, unlike Westerners, the Chinese do not have a history of irreconcilable struggles rooted in the notion of individual freedom and self-reliance. Instead, their culture pattern has always been characterized by mutual dependence: between parents and children, between relatives, between employer and employee, and among fellow villagers and townsmen. Therefore, while white Americans are not averse to receiving governmental benefits via these and other devious means, some of them will inevitably have a guilty conscience and see the relationship as dangerous to their autonomy. One of the reasons for the large generation gap and widespread youthful rebellion is that many American children have decided they can no longer acquiesce in the inconsistencies between their elders' idealistic pronouncements and their opportunistic practices. The Chinese, on the other hand—old and young—are unlikely to concern themselves with the threat to personal autonomy and inconsistencies, and are more likely to easily regard the benefits as part of the order of nature.

Full Participation in the American Dream

If the Chinese and other immigrant and minority groups fix their sights primarily on self-advancement by pursuing the line of least resistance, they will never be fully American. They and their children may become rich and physically comfortable, and they will have contributed to the American society by their physical labor and skills. But they will not have fully participated in the American Dream, for that dream is not merely the acquisition of material wealth in the form of more skyscrapers, more subdivisions, and a bigger share in the Gross National Product (though that is an important part), but the achievement of a just society which can live in peace with the rest of the world, and in which men are freed from oppression and mutual distrust, and where equal opportunities are open to all. It is toward this part of the American Dream that the Chinese in America have yet to aspire and exert themselves. It is upon the realization of this aspect of the American Dream that the American society will ultimately depend for its future, unless we allow the present unsalutary features of American attitudes and behavior characteristics enumerated before—external aggression to enforce American supremacy, internal division due to prejudice and violence, alienation and the decimation of family and kinship—to turn the American Dream into an American Nightmare. What are the Chinese in America doing about the situation?

The Chinese have not, of course, been in America long enough. Since most of them came from humble origins, they simply have not had time to raise their sights to a higher level than limited economic or professional successes.

Then, numerically, Chinese–Americans are insignificant. They constitute the smallest of the minority groups in the United States. Under the circumstances, they are even more likely to be threatened by what Alexis de Tocqueville described as the tyranny of the majority.[8] He spoke of this tyranny in terms of a majority which controls the public force, the judiciary decisions, and legislative processes, and leaves no choice for the minority except abject submission. This tyranny can be especially crippling to some member of the minority whose attempt to make some positive contribution is scornfully spurned by the majority, as the following episode would indicate.

Fong Chow was a Cantonese who came to northern California in the latter part of the nineteenth century during the Gold Rush days. In spite of white prejudice and disabling discrimination, he made a small fortune in his limited way. In appreciation of what his children's school and its teacher had done, Fong spent the colossal sum (for him) of $100 to purchase an elaborately embroidered Chinese silk hanging for a school wall. A storm of protest was raised by the white parents of the mining town, who did not want their children subjected to any aspect of the inferior Chinese cultural influence. Fong's face was temporarily saved when the teacher threatened resignation in mid year if the silk hanging were removed. However, the tapestry and the teacher left the town together at the end of the school year.[9]

The American social and psychological climate in which the minorities find themselves in the 1970's is vastly different from that of Fong Chow in northern California during the Gold Rush days. Unless we are satisfied with things as they are, white Americans as well as minority Americans must proceed on the assumption that the American society is perfectable. In that context, the Chinese in the United States need not feel that they are in any less advantageous position than other groups.

Contribution to the American Dream can be made in large or small packages. For example, the semi-fictional Hakka woman, Char Nyuk Tsin, wife of a leper in the late nineteenth century, whose saga occupied a place in James A. Michener's *Hawaii*, devoted herself for several years not only to serving her dying husband in the leper colony in Molokai, but after his death also worked to transform the leper society from one of total chaos into a sort of organized community. Hers was a selfless dedication of the highest order to a cause which is also exemplified by Western greats from Florence Nightingale to St. Francis Xavier. But, characteristically Chinese, Char Nyuk Tsin devoted the rest of her life to the rearing and betterment of her five sons once she left the abnormal environment of the leper colony. She was not any less admirable for it, but the fact is that the scope of her dedication was defined by kinship and pseudo-kinship.

Another Chinese of humble origin was responsible for the establishment of the Department of Chinese and the Chinese library at Columbia University. In the Gold Rush days, Dean Lung was a domestic in the employ of a naturalized American who was a retired French army general. He was extremely devoted to his employer and his devotion was not shaken by the latter's bad temper and abuse. Instead, he would quote his own half-baked version of Confucian sayings to his erratic employer to explain why he did not leave. One day when Lung's employer asked him what he would like as an expression of his employer's gratitude, Lung replied:

You pay me for my service. I desire for myself nothing more. But United States people know little about Chinese culture and philosophy. Could you do something about that?

Lung's employer made a very large contribution to Columbia University for the establishment of the Chinese department and library. Into that contribution Lung added the sum of $12,000 representing his entire savings from many years' work as a servant. Thereupon, Columbia University also inaugurated the Dean Lung Professorship of Chinese.[10]

We need more Chinese–Americans who will excel not merely in their own crafts and specialties and the amassing of wealth. We need more Chinese who, whatever their occupational endeavors, will apply themselves in earnest and with zeal to the human side of the American Dream. They will not just search for rewards and accolades within the boundaries of the established scheme of things. Instead, they will address themselves to ways and means for realizing the progressive idealism embodied in the American Dream.

It was the vision of our forefathers in the New World that began the American Dream. Throughout American history not all who called themselves Americans were in tune with that dream. In fact, many of them tried their best to destroy it. But it was men and women such as Lincoln, Jefferson, Jackson, John Brown, Harriet Beecher Stowe, Henry David Thoreau, Martin Luther King, Robert Kennedy, Charles Evers, James Earle Fraser,[11] Orestes Brownson,[12] and many others, whose dedication moved the American reality closer to that dream, at least in some respects. These men and women were not all in high places or equally famous. They and others like them are men and women who dared to stand up and be counted on important issues, to dissent and champion unpopular causes at the risk of loss of income, ostracism, or even persecution and jail. Their successors today are speaking up against the Vietnam War and against racial and other injustices at home.[13]

It is easy, in the face of mounting internal and external violence and other problems, to be cynical and say that today we are farther from that Dream than before. Yet, those who care to look will surely realize it is no accident that, as we saw in the previous chapter, the egalitarian patterns of our legal, educational, and social institutions are in sharp contrast to those which prevail in the racist Union of South Africa. Those who are disgusted with American military ventures abroad must at least concede that the change from the pursuit of a purely military victory to a policy of negotiated settlement in Vietnam and the restraints on the use of our enormous powers are directly related to the opposition at home. Did Napoleonic France and Imperial Japan exercise such restraints? Did any European powers in their heyday of colonialism and world-wide expansion exercise restraints with reference to any of the Asian or African peoples they conquered?

The Chinese in America must actively participate in the American Dream by seeking its further realization. In this their Chinese cultural heritage is an advantage and not a liability. In contrast to Whites, they can more easily draw on that heritage for ideas and for behavior patterns which may be instrumental in remedying the defects of the American reality and adding to its progressive idealism. They can more easily take advantage of their ancestral cultural heritage for two reasons. Because they will always be linked with some or all aspects of Chinese culture in the eyes of non-Chinese (whether or not they care for such a linkage), they can speak about the Chinese ways to the non-Chinese public with greater authority. More importantly, since most of them were and will be raised wholly or partly by Chinese parents and grandparents,[14] the Chinese in America cannot help but carry with them some of the content of the Chinese orientation towards men, gods, and things.[15] They can, therefore, more readily attain insight into the Chinese ways and exhibit them behavior-wise. Since they live or were born in America, are raised in American schools, work in the American environment, and read and speak English, they have the opportunity to communicate and enjoy a unique cross-cultural facility for this task.[16]

The problem is not merely to recognize this unique opportunity; having recognized it, will the Chinese in America seize it—to their own advantage and to the advantage of the United States of America with whose future they have, by their American citizenship, identified themselves?

Notes

1. Taken singly, one or another of these elements may be of importance to all politically organized societies. But taken together, the six elements are much more characteristic of many Western societies, including the United States of America, than of most Asian countries, including China. However, the elements making up the second part, to be specified immediately below, are far more uniquely central to the notion of Americanization.

2. Francis L. K. Hsu, *The Study of Literate Civilizations* (New York: Holt, Rinehart and Winston, 1969), p. 61. For a fuller explanation of the postulates, method for deriving postulates, and all the postulates themselves, see pp. 61–83.

3. There are a good many challenges to this postulate, especially by today's alienated young and the militants. But in view of the fact that Congress is still debating from time to time the subject of prayers in public schools and the financial and theological vitality of the churches and seminaries, there is no reason to suspect basic and permanent changes here.

4. Some of these problems are not, of course, peculiar to the United States, nor is the American society the worst sufferer. However, the usual American misconception is that their way of life has eliminated, or is a leader in eliminating, most of them. My work on the American society has led me to the opposite conclusion. To better judge the link between the best of America and the worst, the reader should consult my article, "The Human Equation in Our Future," appended to the end of the book.

5. In these respects, the case of the Chinese in America is quite similar to that of the Japanese minority. As Caudill and DeVos note: "The Japanese Americans provide us, then, with the case of a group who, despite racial visibility and a culture traditionally thought of as alien, achieved a remarkable adjustment to middle class American life because certain compatibilities in the value systems of the immigrant and host cultures operated strongly enough to override the more obvious difficulties" (William Caudill

and George DeVos, "Achievement, Culture and Personality: The Case of the Japanese Americans," *American Anthropologist,* Vol. 58, No. 6 (1956), p. 345. See also William Caudill, *Japanese American Personality and Acculturation,* Genetic Psychology Monographs, Vol. 45 (1952), pp. 3–102. The Japanese culture and tradition are, however, very different from the Chinese in other ways. These are dealt with elsewhere (Francis L. K. Hsu, *Iemoto: The Heart of Japan,* in preparation).

6. Ts'ai T'ing-kai, *Ts-ai T'ing-kai Tze Chuan (Autobiography of Ts'ai T'ing-kai),* Vol. I (Hong Kong: Tzu Yu She [Freedom Press], 1946), pp. 59–63.

7. See Francis L. K. Hsu, *Americans and Chinese: Purpose and Fulfillment in Great Civilizations* (New York: Doubleday and Natural History Press, 1970), Chapter 8.

8. *Democracy in America,* 1948 edition, New York, Alfred A. Knopf, Vol. 1, pp. 259–262.

9. See Theresa A. Sparks, *China Gold* (Fresno, Calif.: Academy Library Guild, 1954), pp. 130–133.

10. S. W. Kung, *Chinese in American Life* (Seattle: University of Washington Press, 1962), p. 234. More recently, an ambitious Institute for Religion and Social Change (based in Honolulu), whose objective is to creatively and critically impart "meaning and purpose to man as he strives to find solutions for the complex and perplexing problems of human development," came into being in 1969 under the leadership of financier–theologian, Hung Wai Ching. However, the significance of this undertaking must be judged by results, which are, of course, yet to come.

11. James Earle Fraser, an Oklahoman (1876–1953), came into contact and played with Indian children between 1880 and 1888. He heard a trapper predict "Indians would be pushed into the Pacific Ocean." He created "End of the Trail," a life size sculpture featuring a worn out Indian warrior on horseback with head bowed, facing the sea. The original is in Cowboy Hall of Fame in Oklahoma City, but a bronze replica of it will be installed in Mooney Grove Park, Visalia, California. His work remained in obscurity for 50 years.

12. Roman Catholic priest who was deeply concerned for the working class and promoted unions and communes.

13. Among others whom we might name are Father Groppi, Benjamin Spock, Dick Gregory, Bob Dylan, Joan Baez, Senators Fulbright, Inouye, and Hatfield, and scores of unsung workers for a greater America whose names may or may not appear in the news media.

14. Some parents are bi-ethnic.

15. Massive confirmation of this point is to be found in a recent article by Kenneth Abbott, "Persistence in Personality and Culture in Chinese Society at Home and Abroad," in George DeVos, ed., *Adaptation, Adjustment, and Culture Change* (in preparation), Chapter 4.

16. It has been observed that third-generation Americans have a tendency to be interested in the language of their ethnic ancestors.

Chinese youngsters demonstrating in San Francisco. (Photo by Gerhard E. Gscheidle/BBM.)

Chapter Eleven

Chinese Identity and the American Dream

Translating needs and goals of large groups or the society as a whole into meaningful patterns of action on the part of the individual is a difficult but not impossible undertaking. In this final chapter, I shall address myself to this question: what should the individual Chinese in America do to make himself more American, to enrich the American Dream, and to facilitate the realization of that dream?

The Importance of China

I must first borrow a page from what has been said about the problem of the Jew in America. According to Kurt Lewin, the basic problem of the Jew is that of group identity. Often repudiated in the country in which he has lived and raised his children for generations, yet having no homeland which he can claim as his own, he suffers from "additional uncertainty," thus giving him "some quality of abnormality in the opinion of the surrounding groups." Lewin concludes that the establishment of a Jewish homeland might "affect the situation of Jews everywhere in the direction of greater normality." [1]

I have discussed Lewin's position more fully elsewhere. [2] The important point which concerns us here is that the condition and activities of the Jews and a Jewish nation quite outside America are intimately linked with how Jewish–Americans feel and are looked upon by non-Jews in America, just as the condition and activities of the Chinese in China cannot help but have an important bearing on how Chinese–Americans feel and are looked upon by non-Chinese in the same environment. It is simply unrealistic for the Chinese in America to divorce their future welfare from what goes on in China; on the contrary, the Chinese in America must concern themselves with China and the Chinese elsewhere.

Lewin's observation about the Jews, however, tells only part of the story. Israel happens to be very friendly with the United States, and is in fact dependent on the latter for its very existence. That is a protector–client relationship which, as we saw before, most white Americans—out of their need to be superior—can wholeheartedly support. But what will transpire if the Jewish homeland and the United States of America do not see eye to eye or are hostile to each other? The logic of Lewin's position leaves no alternative but that such an eventuality would indeed be very harmful to the group identity of the Jewish–American. Unhappily, that is precisely the situation which has befallen the Chinese in America since 1949, due to no fault of their own.

Under the circumstances, the Chinese in America not only have to concern themselves with China but also with improving Sino–United States mutual understanding and trust in order to avoid a military confrontation in which they, along with the rest of mankind, can only lose. They have to concern themselves with these in spite of the racist and intimidating insinuations on the part of such high government officials as J. Edgar Hoover, noted earlier. The Chinese, and other minority groups in similar circumstances, must see such insinuations as obstacles to better American citizenship—obstacles to be overcome and not submitted to. To submit is not only to fail to meet the challenge of the American Dream but to invite worse oppression; individual-centered white Americans have no respect for the meek and those who beg for mercy.

Concern with China and United States–China relations does not mean participating in Chinese politics. In fact, there is good reason to think this would in the long run be harmful to the future of the Chinese in America. It is wrong, in my opinion, for citizens or prospective citizens, of one nation to play politics in another nation. Instead, the Chinese in America can pursue a number of constructive lines of action.

On the one hand, the Chinese can, to protect their group interests, organize themselves in the Jewish model. For example, they can make it impossible for the communications media and entertainers to perpetuate and propagate falsehoods and old prejudices about China and the Chinese—the myth of Chinese expansionism and the treatment of the Chinese in the movie "Thoroughly Modern Millie" are two unequal examples. In addition there is no reason why the Chinese–Americans cannot cooperate with other Asian-Americans or Jewish–Americans to build the substantial political force that each group is unable to generate separately.

On the other hand, the Chinese should help to promote Chinese and Asian studies in the United States on all levels from elementary to graduate school, to arouse interest in China among themselves and among Whites, to disseminate true facts about China and Asia, and to critically evaluate the essence of the Chinese and other Asian civilizations, as well as their significance for the American Dream.

Two lines of pursuit are essential.

There is no question that American schools and universities need curricula that present a much more balanced picture of mankind and its developments than they do today. Americans are accustomed to reading books like *Great Literature of the World* or *Great Paintings of All Time,* which include only Western subject matter. American sociologists still write textbooks on The Family or The Modern Family which deal with only the American family. Some may add one introductory chapter on "The Primitive Family," another on "The Oriental Family," and a third on "The Greek and Roman Family" for window dressing purposes, but they concentrate exclusively on the American scene in the rest of the book when they speak of "The Modern Family." The so-called world history books and courses used to begin with Greek and Roman histories and end with American history. Thanks to the labors of scholars such as Stavrianos and others, we now have some high school and college texts with a somewhat more balanced picture of mankind, but much remains to be done.[3] Should not Chinese–American scholars in the humanities and the social sciences apply themselves to bring about a more balanced picture of mankind?

The other line of pursuit is to cultivate a socially and intellectually broadened condition and atmosphere so that the coming generations of Chinese–Americans will be proud of their Chinese heritage rather than be forced by the pressure of conformity to reject it.

Jewish–Americans keep much of the Jewish tradition alive through their synagogues and synagogue-connected schools. Religious affiliation is more important and definite even among the Japanese than among the Chinese. Having come from a culture in which religion had almost nothing to do with learning, the Chinese in America must depend upon Chinese schools to take the place of Jewish synagogues and Japanese temples. But the Chinese schools in Hawaii and mainland United States, being strapped for financial support, leave much to be desired. Should not Chinese–Americans look into them? We have yet to find a university chair on Chinese studies or a research project relating to China supported entirely by Chinese–American resources. Even the splendid example of the humble Dean Lung has yet to be matched. Is it not time for Chinese–Americans to move themselves in these directions?

Many of the locality associations among the Chinese in America are still based on political divisions of the late Ch'ing dynasty in China, that is, during the time when the first Chinese immigrants came to these shores. Thus there are the Ssu Ta Tu (Si Dai Doo) Association, the Kung Ch'ang Tu (Gung Shang Doo) Association, and many others like them. But the administrative unit *tu* (or *doo*) in China disappeared with the fall of the Manchu dynasty. Should not the Chinese use that fact as an opportunity to regroup in order to achieve more cause-oriented organizations across kinship and locality lines?

Individual Behavior and the American Dream

Aside from this, the Chinese in America have much to contribute as individuals to the human equation in America's future.[4] Only a few examples can be touched on here. One of the basic problems of American society is lack of trust in fellow human beings. This is why laws and regulations have tended to escalate to such an extent that they have a strangulating rather than facilitating effect on progress. The October 1970 report that the federal bureaucracy is defeating the Civil Rights programs is one case in point. But more than that, this lack of trust is fed by the need to test the limit in American interpersonal relations and is in turn necessitated by it. Traditional China went to one extreme of all trust so that laws and regulations were few. Furthermore, even the few laws and regulations were subordinated to the dictates of human relations so that large and impersonal organizations were out of the question. Modern America has gone to the other extreme of all laws and regulations, but the resulting impersonality and the lack of trust threaten to pull the society asunder. Should not the Chinese–American help to moderate the trend, not by telling his white compatriots what to do but by consciously exemplifying his cultural heritage?

The Chinese–Americans have excellent opportunities to contribute to the American Dream in other ways. Coming from a polytheistic heritage, the Chinese in China have never allowed religious belief or church affiliation to set one group of human beings against another. The Chinese in America, as we have seen before, have by and large maintained this approach even though many of them are Christians. They must be less defensive about their Chinese ritual activities connected with ancestor worship and other traditional beliefs. Instead they should better understand the Chinese way in religion and, in connection with any religion, ask themselves and their white friends whether being affiliated with a certain church or performing a certain ritual creates more unity among mankind or more division and strife?

Another area in which the individual Chinese must subject his conduct to careful scrutiny concerns prejudice, racial or otherwise. In 1949 I dined in a downtown Atlanta, Georgia, medium-priced Chinese restaurant where Blacks were served as a matter of course. That was long before Blacks were accepted in any white restaurants or even lunch counters. Throughout the 1940's and 1950's I looked for a Chinese restaurant which did not welcome black patronage. As I traveled from state to state, I did not find one until 1957 in San Francisco. While my wife and I were waiting to be seated in a fancy Chinese restaurant, we noticed several prospective black customers being politely turned away.[5] Superficially, the plush establishment in San Francisco was more Americanized (its owner was probably a favorite Chinese of quite a few of his white customers) because its management acted according to the white majority pattern prevailing at the time. But in the long run, the owners of those Chinese restaurants who did not follow the white majority but served their customers without discrimination contributed more to the realization of the American Dream and were therefore truer Americans.

Each Chinese in America must ask himself: do I, by my words or actions, contribute to racial or religious prejudice in America? Or do I help to reduce it? No Chinese in his right mind can answer the first question in the affirmative and be happy about it unless he is like the ostrich with his head in the sand. It follows that Chinese—and Japanese and other Asians—should serve notice to the Church of the Latter Day Saints that unless its elders change its exclusionist policy concerning Blacks, they will leave its membership too. That will be another contribution to the realization of the American Dream.

Furthermore, the Chinese in America can do other things to reduce prejudice. I have many times heard American-born Chinese girls say they do not consider boys from Taiwan and Hongkong as date prospects at all because they lack sex appeal and social graces. Also I have frequently seen some Chinese scholars and professionals take a very superior air toward most Chinatown-centered Chinese. As a whole, these two groups have little to do with each other. Often the attitude of superiority is explained by its holders on the basis that the behavior of the Chinatowners was at the root of white prejudice. We have seen how unfair the latter view is. Even if the Chinatown-centered Chinese had been innocent of their opium smoking and tong wars, white Americans at the time would have invented other reasons to persecute and exclude them. The Chinese in America must surely see that their exclusion of some categories of Chinese is not different from white exclusion of Chinese. In fact, it is something more; it is Uncle Tomism in yellow skin.

Some older Chinese in America who have suffered from prejudice and carry a degree of white envy often exhibit prejudice in reverse. A Chinese mother of a teen-aged daughter who was going steady with a white classmate said, "You know, his mother even asked me if I mind! Fancy her asking me that!" Then there are not a few Chinese, including some scholars and professionals, who think approval by Whites is the pinnacle of success and tend to automatically respect the opinion of a white colleague much more than that of their fellow Chinese. Each Chinese in America needs to watch himself and try to realize that, in these and other ways, he is unconsciously contributing to the destruction of the American Dream.

Such unconscious prejudices in reverse probably prevent some present or prospective Chinese–American politician from even thinking about a nonracial basis of power. He should reflect on the fact that had Senator Brooke relied primarily on the black vote and President Kennedy on a Catholic constituency, neither of these men would have assumed office. Racial and religious prejudice cannot be combated effectively unless Americans root out the unconscious as well as the conscious ramifications of that prejudice. For this reason those Chinese who think that they cannot really be more active because they are numerically so small are destructive of the American Dream by default. Retention of racial barriers and racial quotas are not part of the American Dream. On the contrary, the success of the American Dream depends on cooperation across all sorts of barriers, including the racial. There is no reason why Chinese cannot get together with Asians, Africans, and the large number of white Americans who actively try to foster the realization of the American Dream, not destroy it.

There is, however, one area of prejudice which the Chinese in America, because of their cultural heritage, cannot help but moderate. This is the generation gap, two expressions of which are the equation of old age with obsolescence and the identification of youth with rebellion and alienation, or unquestioned progress and unmitigated idealism. It is necessary for us to realize that blanket categorization and frozen attitudes toward whole groups are really the foundation of all prejudices. The Chinese–Americans have not contributed to prejudice in these areas because, by and large, they still respect the aged. The Chinese adolescent, except a small number of militants (including some new arrivals from Hongkong who have come to join their laboring parents in Chinatowns after long years of separation), have not yet as a whole exhibited any significant tendency to pull away from their elders and join the ranks of the rebels and the alienated.[6] There is no mystery about this. Having come from a cultural heritage in which the maintenance of the human network is more important than personal satisfaction, the Chinese parent tends to see less competition in his children's achievement, and more continuity and fulfillment. When parents do not need to hold on to children, children have less need to tear themselves free. At the same time, thoroughly accepting the notion that human beings depend upon each other, the Chinese parents and children tend to devote more energy to mutual assistance rather than mutual avoidance or recrimination.

The Chinese in America, coming from a prolonged cultural history of passive acquiescence toward political authority and of personal advancement through zigzagging but realistic adjustments to obstacles, still tend to shun causes and avoid open confrontations. There is a well-known saying attributed to a Chinese scholar–official of the 6th century B.C.: "When the government is oppressive, one must walk gingerly and speak very little." Throughout the last two millennia, Chinese tea houses and restaurants always posted on their premises the following signs: "Not responsible for your belongings" and "Do not discuss national affairs."

When men dare not speak up on important matters which affect their very existence, they will acquire an attitude of apathy and noninvolvement about many things. This is commensurate with another Chinese saying: "To get involved in one thing more is not as good as one thing less." This is at least part of the background which led the Chinese in America to give themselves rarely to causes, especially unproven and prestigeless causes. This is also why intellectual conversations are not usually part of the dinner fare, even at gatherings of Chinese scholars and professionals in America.

Hence, I was pleasantly surprised when I recently (1970) read some letters to the editor of the *Honolulu Advertiser* by Hawaiian-born Chinese (and Japanese) college students expressing their views on the controversial anti-establishment demonstrations at Yale University and on other matters. Over the years, I have seen few public expressions of concern on controversial issues by Chinese–Americans, either in letters to editors or elsewhere. The coming generations of Chinese and the Chinese elders must see such expressions not only as their legitimate right but also as their necessary duty as Americans—as Americans who want actively to contribute to the American Dream and not Americans who merely reap its benefits in passivity.

A Positive Approach to Double Identity

In assuming a positive attitude toward Americanization, the Chinese in America need, however, to keep in mind one note of caution: *complete* Americanization to the extent of total similarity with white Americans is impossible. This is not merely because Chinese (and other Asians) are as a whole physically distinguishable from Whites, as Calvin Lee emphasizes.[7] That is obvious enough. But even when racial differences are absent, as between the Chinese and the Thais, in a society where 50 to 80 percent of the host population have, through generations of intermarriage, some Chinese ancestry, Chinese identity has not disappeared. Superficially, at least, one reason for this may seem to be that the Chinese have a sense of cultural superiority vis-à-vis the Thais.[8] Given a situation where the Chinese are actively attracted to the ways of the host population, will they submerge their minority identity more readily?

I do not think this will come about for two reasons. One, the Chinese identity will be buttressed not so much by any alleged Chinese sense of cultural superiority as by the greater security and satisfaction the individual can derive within the Chinese matrix of social relations than outside it. The other reason is directly linked with the first one. Once again we have to borrow a page from the situation of the Jews in America for illustration. There are many Jewish youngsters in America who are raised as non-Jews. They do not observe Jewish customs and are not affiliated with Jewish temples. Our available evidence indicates that such youngsters have a much harder time adjusting to their peers in college than those who have been raised consciously and militantly to cultivate their identity in the Judaic tradition and temple life. In other words, even though most Jews are white and not distinguishable from most other Whites, their complete identity and assimilation as Americans are always subject to rejection.[9]

This tallies well with the need of white Americans to assert their superiority as a defense against their fear of inferiority, a fear we noted in the previous chapter. If physical differences are not available for discrimination, other grounds will be found, indeed will be created to satisfy that need. The

American college student of Jewish ancestry who was not brought up self-consciously as a Jew was again and again the object of the quizzy and somewhat derogatory remark on the part of non-Jewish Whites: "what's he trying to hide?" This white American attitude as a barrier to complete assimilation of all minority groups is likely to persist in the foreseeable future.[10]

This means that the Chinese in America, in common with other minority groups, will have a continuing problem of double identity. But the effective way of dealing with it is not to deny its existence but to face it squarely.[11] The first step is to realize that the double identity of a minority group is not dissimilar to that of the professional woman. She is a woman and a professional. Some American professional women have tended to forget about their sex identity but most have kept some sort of balance between it and their profession. In the latter case, their sex identity sometimes becomes an advantage rather than a disability.

To achieve this balance, the Chinese in America will do best if he knows Chinese as a second language or at least will take the trouble to familiarize himself with aspects of Chinese history and culture, and additionally to concern himself with China, especially with reference to her relations with the United States. There is every advantage for the Chinese in retaining something of a Chinese identity culturally and in human relations, but at the same time, being more American in politics and in professional life. Of course, they need not, they should not, and they cannot keep these two identities completely separate from each other. On the contrary, they are bound to bring something of the American strengths into their social and cultural life, and infuse something of the Chinese touch into their political and professional participation. This is how the American Dream may be enriched and one of the ways in which Americans as a whole may come nearer its realization.

Of course, double identity does complicate one's life somewhat. But in the American context it offers a wide range of possibilities depending upon individual initiative and predilection. Quite a few anthropologists have begun to develop a concept of America as a pluralistic society. That, too, can be part of the American Dream. Should not the Chinese and members of other minorities, each with a double identity, play an ever greater role in a social fabric where many strands of people work together but where racial, religious, and other identities are not the overwhelming factors for privileges or disabilities?

In their search for balance, the Chinese in America must surely realize that no society has ever been absolutely good, free, or just, nor is such a society ever likely to appear on this earth. They have had to contend with white prejudice, it is true. But their forefathers in China had to contend with many more obstacles, including frequent destruction by contending warlords and foreign invasions and a social and economic framework that set more confining limits on the individual.

Perhaps one of the mechanisms for the evolution toward such a pluralistic society is for all Americans consciously to be grouped with labels showing their separate ethnic identities, not just the minority groups. We have Spanish–Americans, Afro–Americans, Chinese–Americans; why not Swedish–Americans, Irish–Americans, Italian–Americans, and Russian–Americans? It is true that white Americans are sometimes identified according to ethnic origin, but only for such special occasions as a Swedish–American Day. What we must look forward to is a situation where all Americans are equally so designated, beginning with the census and all official records. Such labels will then fulfill a *positive* need in the individual's psychological functioning in a more truly pluralistic social system, not merely a defensive device for the retention of cultural identity defined by racists as inferior. The arguments for this are as sound as those for school integration.[12]

As members of a minority group in America with wider cultural vision and experiences than most white Americans, the Chinese in America know well that those who hope for the realization of absolutes—absolute good, absolute freedom, absolute justice—are easily disillusioned. They are in a better position to know, too, that those who, upon becoming disillusioned with America's imperfections, have gone overboard to embrace another system are in for greater shocks when confronted by still greater imperfections in the cause they have newly espoused.

For this reason, Americans with double identity and insight into two cultural traditions can help the dissatisfied Americans to take a good look at the basis, implications, and potentialities of a way of life too often taken for granted. They can also help the completely satisfied Americans better appreciate the real dangers and pitfalls of a way of life which has given them so much and which they hope to preserve, so that, together, the two groups might develop better avenues not only for its preservation but also for its advancement.

Assessment of Americanization

The following brief schematic view may help us to clarify our thoughts on the subject of Americanization. It is organized around three key concepts which I think are basic to the American Dream: *Resources, Identity,* and *Ideal.* In connection with *Resources,* the individual should ask himself: "Do I have the opportunity to make full use of my potentialities?" In connection with *Identity,* he should ask: "What are the reasons why I am proud of being a Chinese–American (or Polish–American or Afro–American)?" Finally, in connection with *Ideal,* he should ask: "In what way am I, by word or deed, advancing or retarding the building of a more perfect society in which all Americans will not only live better materially but also have greater trust in each other?"

The items listed in each column are not ranked and not exhaustive but

The American Dream and the Minority

Resources		Identity		Ideal	
A. Livelihood	B. Protection	A. Group	B. Individual	A. Contributive	B. Detrimental

1. Material Reward
  (a) Money
  (b) Freedom of choice (occupation, profession, or area of operation)
2. Social Reward
  (a) Freedom of choice in residence, association, and cemetery
  (b) Deserved recognition
	1. Equality before the law
	
	2. Security of person and property
		1. Majority view of the minority group's life and history: reality versus prejudice
		2. Minority view of the minority group's life and history: reality versus prejudice
		3. Assimilation without annihilation
			1. Excellence in work
			2. Degree of social acceptance
			3. Problem of self-esteem
			4. Problem of envy of majority
			5. Problem of models
				1. Excellence in work
				2. Courage to dissent
				3. Active political participation
				4. Combating prejudice in words and deeds
				5. Commitment to change within the constitutional framework
					1. Uncle Tomism
					2. Violence
					3. Corruption of public officials for gainful ends
					4. Prejudice against those less favorably situated

embody the central relevant points. There is obviously a degree of relatedness between columns. The reader who is a member of a minority group can use this tabulation to gauge where he and his ethnic group stand and in what areas they need to direct their efforts, just as one who is a white American can use it to appreciate how far he and his ethnic group are helping the minority Americans and themselves to work toward a fuller realization of the American Dream.

Perhaps neither the minorities in America nor those in majority groups will ever be able to claim complete realization of the American Dream. That is, of course, the nature of all visions of the future. But it is also the nature of visions to inspire those who possess them. In this, the Chinese–American (and other minority Americans) can do a great deal.

Notes

1. Kurt Lewin, "Psycho-Sociological Problems of a Minority Group," in *Character and Personality* Vol. III (1935), pp. 175–187. Reprinted in Kurt Lewin, *Resolving Social Conflict* (New York: Harper and Brothers, 1948).

2. Francis L. K. Hsu, "American Core Value and National Character," in *Psychological Anthropology,* Francis L. K. Hsu, ed. (Homewood, Ill.: Dorsey Press, 1961), pp. 225–228.

3. See Lefton S. Stavrianos, et. al., *A Global History of Man* (Boston: Allyn and Bacon, 1964) and my analysis of the content of this book and of Anatole G. Mazur and John M. Peoples' *Men and Nations: A World History* (New York: Harcourt, Brace and World, 1964) in Francis L. K. Hsu, *Americans and Chinese: Purpose and Fulfillment in Great Civilizations, op. cit.,* pp. 95–97.

4. See the Appendix to this book, "The Human Equation in Our Future."

5. It has since 1960 changed the rule to "all are welcome," as have a majority of white-owned restaurants throughout the nation. Dr. Alexander DeConde informs me that he knew of Chinese restaurants in Washington, D.C., that refused services to Blacks in the 1940's. There were undoubtedly others like them before the 1960's.

6. Some Chinese parents see too much generation gap between themselves and their children already. Partly this is because of the inevitable difference between their own experiences as children and those experienced as parents. But it seems to me that some Chinese parents think and talk about the generation gap because it is fashionable in view of the white context. In realistically assessing the extent of the generation gap among the Chinese–Americans, one must keep strictly to the comparative perspective. That is to say, compared with Whites, the Chinese–Americans still have little of it. This gap is not even too evident among parents with militant children. I have personally known a few very ultra-militant Chinese college students; sometimes I have known their parents, as well. I cannot but sense a kind of pride of achievement on the latters' part. The old are not unhappy to see their children's names and pictures in the papers and the young gloat over their doings as though silently shouting, "Look, Ma, no hands." It may seem fantastic to some readers, but in today's America and to some people, campus fame through militancy is almost a new kind of "Dean's List."

7. Calvin Lee, *Chinatown, U.S.A.* (Garden City, N.Y.: Doubleday & Co., 1965), p. 143.

8. Richard J. Coughlin, *Double Identity, The Chinese in Modern Thailand* (Hongkong: Hongkong University Press, 1960), pp. 198–199.

9. Samuel Teitelbaum, *Patterns of Adjustment among Jewish Students,* Northwestern University, Ph.D. dissertation, 1953, unpublished.

10. My research helper, Mrs. Adele Andelson, who is Jewish, believes that "today, such Jewish youngsters who have no religious training do not find it difficult to adjust to their peers in college; they have less difficulty than their parents." I agree with her in one respect. There is evidence that among youths who form communes or otherwise are actively anti-establishmentarian, traditional differences such as ethnic origin tend to be totally irrelevant. But these developments have also led to a degree of polarization on campuses so that the anti-anti-establishmentarians tend to intensify their need for old dividers of men.

11. I have met successful professional Hawaiian Chinese who scoff at this statement. One such man said, "This question of the Chinese identity issue is going to be dead in 25 years! Or even in five years." As if to supply a reason for the first speaker, a second successful man said, "Hawaiian Chinese are different. We simply are different from those Chinatown Chinese." I have met successful Japanese–Americans in Hawaii who would thoroughly agree with these statements. Professional or business success reduces the problem of identity of the minority but does not eliminate it.

12. I first advanced this view in a lecture at the Lee Family Association of Hawaii on April 22, 1970. I was very pleased later to receive this same suggestion from Dr. Kenneth A. Abbott.

Appendix

The Human Equation in our Future[1]

I

In 1960 a Committee on National Goals was appointed by President Eisenhower. The results of this committee's work were summarized in a speech entitled "Our Goal: Individualism or Security?" at Bowdoin College by its chairman, Dr. Henry Wriston, President Emeritus of Brown University. This most eloquent précis, extolling the rugged individual, maintained that the greatness of a country depends upon its leadership, and leadership cannot be stimulated and nurtured without rugged individualism. The popular importance of such a concept is shown in the frequency with which the speech was reprinted, in part or wholly, in the *Chicago Sun-Times* (June 5, 1960), the *Wall Street Journal* (June 1, 1960), *Reader's Digest* (August 1960), and elsewhere. Some papers even endorsed Wriston's view in editorials.

Wriston's views were not only echoed by the former Lebanese Foreign Minister, Charles Malik—a public speaker much in demand in the United States—at Williamsburg, Virginia, in a widely publicized speech June 11, 1960, commemorating the fifty-day prelude to Independence Day, but were praised by most of the eight prominent men who contributed to *Life* magazine's series "The National Purpose" (May 23 through June 20, 1960, issues).

The 1960 wave of self-examination manifested itself when our innumerable internal problems were already evident, and many people were concerned with our failure to top Russia in space exploration. Now, ten years later, while we have indeed mastered space, we are tragically and divisively mired in an Asian land war, our internal problems have intensified, and a new sense of urgency and a new wave of self-examination would seem to be in order.

However, while I see signs of this sense of urgency, I do not see any indication of self-examination of the human values which Americans consider to be part of the order of nature. I see preoccupation with environmental pollution, read about economic and legal measures to reduce racial tension and violence, and hear visionary but materialistic prescriptions for the future well-being of our country. But I do not see any critical interest in that basic ingredient of human existence—man's pattern of relationship with his fellow men.

To be sure, we must reduce pollution, find mitigating factors to lower the violence level, and develop systematic insights into the future. A distinguishing mark of man is his ability to project into the unknown. However, science must proceed from the known to the unknown, not vice versa; and the science of man's future, as distinguished from a fantasy, must follow the same rules.

All individuals must live as part of some human group. Children who reject their parents seek the company of peers. Most lovers of solitude are in reality anxious to be discovered.

II

Given this fundamental assumption, I frankly see our society today as suffering from a crisis in interpersonal relationships, due to rugged individualism, even as I readily admit that many (though not all) of the strengths of the American way of life are related to this same individualism.

Western man has attained his superiority over the rest of the world during the last 300 years not by way of his religion or his romantic love but by dint of his ideologies, his science and technology, and his organizational fervor and skill. His self-reliant ideology led him to discard the shackles of paternal authority, monarchical power, and medieval magic in favor of wider organizations such as national states, both democratic and totalitarian, and universalist churches and industrial empires. When the West met Africa and the East, it was the Western man's scientific technology and well-organized armed might which subdued or dominated the rest of the world.

While ideology, science and technology, and organization are three of the outstanding contributions of contemporary Western man to the world, their very psychological foundation is unfortunately a factor in Western man's difficulties with himself and with his fellow man. It is the burden of this presentation that all of our major problems—from the generation gap and alienation to corruption in business and government, from racial and religious prejudice to interpersonal and group violence—are directly or indirectly traceable to that much extolled virtue of our Founding Fathers, rugged individualism.

The basic ingredient of rugged individualism is militant self-reliance, but here we must briefly distinguish between self-reliance under rugged individualism and self-reliance cum self-sufficiency under other circumstances.

Adulthood in any society indicates a degree of self-reliance; that is, adults are better able to take care of their physical and mental needs than children. But American rugged individualism means that one must strive toward self-reliance as a life goal. The individual should constantly tell himself and others that he controls his own destiny and that he does not need help or sympathy. A university friend once told me he was puzzled by a militant colleague. The university was involved in a faculty-student dispute, so common on campus today, about curriculum revision. The colleague told my friend he did not care what lousy curriculum was decided upon as long as he was involved in the decision process. This is extreme rugged individualism in action.

An intercultural comparison will also clearly illustrate the point. Suppose a hard-working man in traditional China had not had many material goods all his adult life, but in his old age his sons were able to provide for him generously. He would not only be happy, but he would be likely to let the world know how his good children were supporting him in a style to which he had never been accustomed. To the contrary, an American parent in similar circumstances would be ashamed of himself and would resent any reference to such a situation; an American who is not self-reliant is considered a misfit, a dependent character who is thought to be in need of psychiatric help.

The rugged individual's self-reliance has two attributes: the first is fierce competitiveness and the second is aggressive creativity. I shall demonstrate some negative consequences of rugged individualism so that readers may judge for themselves.

III

First let us discuss sexual morality, even though such a subject seems terribly outmoded today. But let us not consider it in any absolute and universal sense, for what is moral at one time or in one society may be immoral at another time or in another society. We must look at American standards and proceed from there. According to American custom, pre-marital and extra-marital sex, wife-swapping, prostitution, promiscuity, and the sale and viewing of pornography are all immoral; yet all of these have been on the increase.

For example, about ten years ago the Postmaster General disclosed that "mail-order pornography and obscenity is a $500 million-a-year business that is growing in volume." One of the reasons, the official said, was "the tremendous profit realized from a relatively small capital investment." [2]

Now it is perfectly true that smut sales by mail can result in tremendous profits from a relatively small capital investment, but if a society enjoins the individual to compete by creative efforts for success on individualistic terms, what would be more natural for him than to aim at tremendous profits from a small capital investment? Are not some of the best American success stories based on such entrepreneurship? American business always says: give the customer what he wants. Therefore, if consumer research so indicates, is it not good business to provide more blatant sex?

Mail-order smut is only a small part of the total picture. A Chicago minister, Chairman of the Legislative Committee of the Churchman's Commission for Decent Publications, observed that the tide of smut was "directly responsible for an alarming breakdown of moral fiber in this country." The minister said the magazines, if read by any youth, would give him a fairly accurate blueprint of "... how to seduce a virgin; how to rape a girl; how to take advantage of the absence of a husband or wife in order to have illicit sex relations; how to prime a girl with liquor to make her receptive to sexual relations; how to use torture to heighten sexual feelings, and so on." [3] Even ten years ago, when the minister made these observations, youth did not have to depend on publications, and today sex is ubiquitous. Young people can see award-winning movies; they can learn from the highly glamorized supposedly clandestine sex lives of their movie idols and public performers. Above all, they and their parents are under pressure to find creative ways of self-fulfillment, and like the professor who did not care about the results of the decision so long as he was doing the deciding, the rugged individual under other circumstances can simply say his own enjoyment is more important than social consequences.

The next correlate of rugged individualism is corruption and dishonesty in government and business, which are nothing new in any large and complex society. What is unusual is that the wealthiest country on earth should be rife with sharp practices and chicanery.

We think competition is governed by rules and chivalry, but do not realize that for every lucky one who succeeds, thousands do not; since failure means loss of self-respect, competition is often a matter of dog eat dog. We think creativity involves scientific advances and artistic achievements, but do not acknowledge that another definition of creativity is deviation from the norm and the law. When the rugged individual is forced into a corner, we cannot blame him for failing to live up to his principles.

This is why, although theft and robbery are prevalent and costly, more prevalent and costlier still are what sociologists call white-collar crime—misrepresentation in financial statements of corporations, manipulation in stock exchanges, commercial bribery, bribery of public officials to secure favorable contracts and legislation, misrepresentation in advertising and salesmanship, embezzlement and misapplication of funds, short weights and measures, misgrading of commodities, tax frauds, and misapplication of funds in receiverships and bankruptcies—all covered by what Al Capone would describe as "the legitimate rackets." [4] Thus in the main, corruption in America is not rooted in poverty. It is frequently committed in vast proportions by people who are well-fed and well-clothed but who must find creative ways to expand and enlarge their operations in order to compete with others for greater success.[5]

Opponents of this view may say that those who resort to corruption to obtain greater success have misused creativity and competition. My answer is that when individual success is given a primary honored place in life, there is little room left for any workable criteria by which wholesome creative and competitive efforts can be distinguished from unwholesome ones.

A third correlate of rugged individualism, conformity, is in direct and paradoxical opposition to its avowed aim. In fact, the label conformity is so repugnant to the rugged individual that it prompted David Riesman to see Americans as changing from their original "Inner-directed" personality orientation to an "Other-directed" one.[6] Riesman erred because he failed to see the real link between rugged individualism and conformity.

We noted previously that a basic ingredient of rugged individualism is militant self-reliance, but we also noted that the very foundation of the human way of life is man's participation in some human group, without which we should have no custom, no art, no science, no law, and not even language. Human existence demands mutual dependence among human beings intellectually, socially, emotionally, and technologically. But that basic American value, aggressive self-sufficiency, denies the importance of other human beings in one's life and creates contradictions which engender personal insecurity.

The central feature of this insecurity is the lack of permanency not only in one's ascribed relationships but also in one's achieved relationships. There is an insistent demand on the individual to be unceasing in his efforts to surpass his fellow men but at the same time to seek their company in status-giving groups. For both purposes—status-improvement and status-maintenance—the individual must possess unequivocally the accepted signs and symbols of belonging to a given group. In other words, in order to live up to the ideal of militant self-reliance, Americans are forced to do exactly the opposite. Expressed in the jargon of science, there is a direct relationship between rugged individualism and conformity: the stronger the emphasis on rugged individualism, the greater the individual need for conformity.[7]

Evidence for this theory is abundant, but none is more interesting than that given in a summary report on the "Cornell Study of Student Values," which covered a total of 2,760 undergraduate men and women attending Cornell and 4,585 undergraduate men and women attending ten universities (UCLA, Dartmouth, Fisk, Harvard, Michigan, North Carolina, Texas, Wayne, Wesleyan, and Yale). Edward S. Suchman, the author, concluded: "Much of the student's development during four years in college does *not* take place in the classroom. The conformity, contentment, and self-centered confidence of the present-day American students are not academic values inculcated by the faculty, but rather the result of a highly organized and efficiently functioning extracurricular social system."[8]

This leads us to a fourth correlate: prejudice. It is curious that a culture which extols Christian love, freedom, equality, and democracy should be plagued by racism and religious bigotry, but this contradiction may be easily resolved in light of our analysis. In an extremely mobile society, the rugged individual is anxious to look above for opportunities to climb, but at the same time he is threatened by encroachments from below and is forced to conform either to the customs of the group of which he is already a member or to which he aspires. Associating with members of a less prestigious group is a sure way of losing status. The backbone of prejudice is, therefore, conformity rooted in the fear of inferiority, rather than inherent wickedness of bigots. Bigots may utilize intolerance to obtain votes in an election, resort to physical violence against members of minority groups to keep them in place, or use devious methods to keep them from job opportunities. But militant bigots are always the minority, and they can only achieve success if fear of inferiority is prevalent among the silent majority which they try to inflame.

The fifth correlate of rugged individualism is isolation of the individual. This philosophy forces men to keep not only their thoughts but particularly their feelings from each other; they dare not be off guard with one another. For fear of rejection they have no one except psychiatrists or modern-day Dorothy Dixes on whom they can unload their conscious or unconscious anxieties. To avoid the onus of charity they decline help and sympathy from friends and relatives.

But a human condition in which one can be off guard, take the opportunity to unload his anxieties, and fulfill the need to receive succor—these are the true measure of human intimacy, which the American way discourages. Intimacy becomes such a scarce commodity that many seek salvation in improved communication. But the prior condition for communication is the willingness to communicate and be communicated to; when that condition is lacking, fine tools of communication are not only powerless to reduce human mistrust but excellent disguises for psychological distance.

Isolation of the individual leads to a variety of consequences, only two of which can be dealt with here. The first is suspicion and then fear of one's fellow men; the second is the need to resort to defensive action to strengthen his personal success and security. He will resort to or condone violence if he deems it necessary. And he easily expands his ego so that he may want to make the world safe for Christianity (or capitalism, Communism, Whites, or whatever).

Ecstasy in the rugged individual's successes and misery in his failures are equally great, for they cannot be shared. Therefore, while the resources and opportunities remain unlimited, some rugged individuals may manage to live in peace with others. But if the resources and opportunities demand competition, one man's gain is viewed as another man's loss.

In every society the generation gap exists because of the difference in age and experiences between old and young. But if the maturity and independence of children leave parents no place in the children's scheme of things to come, and children see parents as stumbling blocks to their manhood and womanhood, a greatly intensified generation gap is inevitable. In every society, people who are in direct competition with each other for anything are not likely to love each other. Bloody court intrigues in the old world come readily to mind, but thanks to the democratizing process of America we now have the court intrigue psychology on such a nationwide scale that human trust is a rare commodity.

Americans often note with satisfaction that under totalitarian regimes men fear to confide in each other because of secret police. But we do not realize that we tend to be secretive about ourselves because of rugged individualism. When men do not trust each other, they become suspicious of each other's intentions. They find the human environment unpredictable, for everything is subject to change without notice. Friendship becomes temporary, so that illustrious careers are sometimes reached by roads littered with the bodies of old friendships.

Yet, as we have pointed out, man cannot live alone, for to be human is to be a member of some human group. The rugged individual is compelled to take one or all of the following approaches to interpersonal relations: he tries to buy his way into a relationship with his fellow human beings. He pays for their usefulness and is repaid for his utility. They do not relate and cannot in fact divulge their feelings for one another. The United States attitudes do not permit men to be sentimental about each other, and physical intimacy must be avoided. Or, he builds what Edward T. Hall calls invisible "bubbles" around himself. All human beings are separated from one another by psychological space. Regardless of time and place, there is always mental material that one wishes to keep private. But the rugged individual not only keeps much to himself; he goes to extraordinary lengths to project an image of himself quite different from reality. Nowadays institutions use public relations consultants to do this. However, we do not often realize how far the American individual can go in using public relations techniques. Deodorants are popular so that we can keep our smells from each other.

This large psychological distance between men was discussed by the social psychologist Kurt Lewin in his book *Resolving Social Conflict*.[9] Lewin, a German expatriate, found differences between Germany and the United States in interpersonal relations. A newcomer to a German community will not get to know anybody for a long time, but once he does he will share deeper confidences. A newcomer to a community in the United States will immediately find friends, but that friendship will often stagnate at the most superficial levels no matter how long he remains there.

Finally, the rugged individual is most in tune with a crisis psychology. Rugged individuals will unite to an extraordinary extent if there is a common threat, and into this feverish unity he can release his pent-up feelings, and through this intense unity he can enjoy a kind of intimate camaraderie with members of the same sex which he has been missing.[10] Moreover, the common threat does not have to have a particular quality, name or shape: it may be Communism, Islam, Jews, Chinese, Catholics, Blacks, Unidentified Flying Objects, integration, hippies, teetotalers, animal lovers or haters, ad infinitum. If there is no ready-made enemy, make one up; there must be an enemy, for to fight the enemy is good for the soul.

Since offense is the best defense, rugged individuals will not stop at a nuclear Great Wall. It takes no effort at all for rugged individuals to pursue war; the next one will usually be a war to make the world safe for peace lovers. And as to what some rugged individuals have in mind within the society, let us briefly quote the report of the chief of Veterans of Foreign Wars before state VFW officials at a recent appearance in Jefferson City, Missouri, February 28, 1970:

The national commander of the VFW said yesterday the United States might have to resort to a police state to contain the militant left wing. . . .

[The commander concluded] I hate to see this country develop into some type of police state, but, to have security for our people, it may be necessary.[11]

This complex psychology of the rugged individual has a special bearing on the shape of international relations. The rugged individual wants to mold the world in his image. He sets out to advance himself by overcoming all obstacles. He is prepared to gain his ends by submitting to conformity if necessary, but with reference to those deemed inferior to him, he demands conformity to his wishes. He may go to great trouble and expense to take care of his inferiors, help them, educate them, and reform them, *as long as they acknowledge their inferiority and do his bidding.* The most intolerable situation exists when those he considers inferior demand equality, or even worse, act superior. Since the ultimate goal of the rugged individual is preeminence over all, he will resort to hostility and violence to defend his alleged superiority.

We come now to a final correlate, another paradox, which is organization. At the beginning we noted how organization was a strength of the Western man vis-á-vis the rest of the world. But we are not always aware of the pernicious effects of organization on man, the best account of which is found in William H. Whyte's *The Organization Man.*[12] Having correctly analyzed the effects of organization, Whyte merely concludes with the suggestion that the individual fight organization. How can the individual fight organization without more organization? Whyte shares with many others the same fallacy, that organization and rugged individualism are diametrically opposed to each other. This is why he advised the individual to fight organization, for Whyte did not challenge the soundness of rugged individualism as the final guiding principal of man.

Human life is impossible without organization. Rousseau's famous dictum that man is born free, but is everywhere in chains, is as unsound as the idea that the earth is flat. Were we truly free we would be like wild animals. Organization involves definite lines of demarcation between peoples and their actions. We find men and women living together out of wedlock who fulfill all the requirements of marriage, but society needs a clear distinction between those who are married and those who are not. We find healers who are more effective than doctors but the laws must be precise to distinguish between those who are graduates of certified medical schools and those who are not. Individuals are classified as legitimate or illegitimate, employed or unemployed, male or female, and in a thousand other ways. Many of these classifications are arbitrary, but they are indispensable in any society.

However, the amount of organization is in direct ratio to the complexity of the society and, within complex societies, in direct ratio to the emphasis upon rugged individualism. The first part of this formula is self-evident; the second section needs further elaboration.

Let us examine the problem of smut sales. More severe competition will force the purveyors of obscenity into more creative means to get more trade. The government is imperceptibly forced into more organizational means to censor, regulate, apprehend, and punish the culprits who have gone too far. The same situation exists with regard to corruption and dishonesty. More severe competition will inevitably compel more individuals and corporations into more creative means to reach greater success. Potential embezzlers and confidence men will seek new ways to defraud the company or the public. Syndicates and corporations will hire experts to seek loopholes in the law and find new avenues to influence public officials. Ultimately the government is forced to proliferate its laws and widen its organization to protect the public interest and the national welfare.

The most unusual development, yet most understandable in the light of our analysis, is found in American religion. Our churches have taken on every characteristic of big business. This big business psychology has gone so far that we seem to forget that religion is a personal matter, a private relationship between the individual and his god. On the contrary, we are led to believe that outside the organized church there is no salvation and only those who are members of an organized parish possess a direct link with God. How far this big business mentality has permeated the church is indicated by a *Christian Century Magazine* survey of 1951 (based on the results of a poll of 100,000 ministers all over the country) to determine the "outstanding" and most "successful" churches in the United States. The results showed twelve to be deserving of such merit and praise.

One of these was the First Presbyterian Church of Hollywood. A report on this most "successful" church in *Reader's Digest* (February 1952) described the size of its membership, organization, budget, and physical plant; the number of clubs, choirs, and basketball teams; its radio and TV programs; cordons of prayer, pushbutton-like card files, and kitchen facilities, but little about the quality of the minister's teachings. In other words, the "success" of this church seemed to consist of the organizational endeavors of the parishioners that rebounded to their benefit alone and a whirl of competitive activity which was inferentially equated with depth of spiritual faith.

Since then, two sociologists, Louis Schneider and Sanford M. Bornbusch, reviewed a total of 46 best sellers on religion in America over an eighty-year period (1875–1955).[13] Their findings leave no doubt about the accuracy of the *Reader's Digest* analysis.

My intention here is not to criticize the church as such, since I am a social analyst and not a reformer. However, I do wish to suggest that competition and creativity tend to undermine the true foundation of religion; churchmen have no alternative but to resort to organizational methods and public relations devices to keep people interested.

IV

For purposes of this presentation, I have made no value judgments. My task is to point out the possible links between the much extolled rugged individualism and many facts which have never been so linked. It does not mean that, because of rugged individualism, a majority of the American people are active parties to the consequences just outlined. Even if all laws were thrown overboard, a majority of us would remain law-abiding. But in such an eventuality the unlawful activities would increase and make life less tenable for that law-abiding majority. Most citizens of our society would remain decent and honest in spite of cutthroat competition. But a great increase of such competition would push the rest of us to the brink so that we, too, would be liable to the same pitfalls, and our society as a whole would head in the opposite direction from that it ideally intends.

We may ask if rugged individualism helped to catapult Westerners to their prominence in today's world, why can't it do the same in the world of tomorrow? The answer must be sought in an elementary anthropological discovery: that human beings, their ideologies, technologies, and organizational methods operate in social and cultural contexts which determine not only their meanings but also their results.

Eighteenth- and nineteenth-century American individualism was indeed more rugged than its English counterpart. The scope of equality and freedom was widened in this society to cover the economic and social as well as the political aspects of life. But although the United States early abolished aristocracy and frowned upon class hierarchy, yet the church, old world traditions, the solidarity of the small local community, and the expanding frontier still served as checks on the wanton exercise of rugged individualism or as outlets for it.

However, as the sociologist George Homans has found, rugged individualism has so decimated our small-town life that it no longer exercises the same kind of social control it originally did.[14] The population explosion everywhere and rising nationalism in the non-Western world have radically reduced the open frontiers to which the rugged individual can go. He has examined the moon and found it unpromising for suburbia. He has nowhere to go except to advance himself at the expense of others in this increasingly crowded world.

Individualism has helped to bring about great things in the world, but the conditions of life in which this value and ideal has served its ends effectively have changed. A new human equation is necessary for our survival, and in this new human equation we must be prepared to modify the value we hold so dear—or even eliminate it if need be. In working toward this new equation we must ask, what are civilizations for?

Anthropologists have long taught cultural relativism, but in one aspect my view is not relativistic. That is, civilizations—whether they give us philosophies, moral rules, profits, air conditioning, or clean sheets—exist for men and not vice versa. Those who glibly speak of industrial imperatives to which men must adjust do not realize how far they agree with totalitarian mentalities for whom the state supersedes the individual. But if civilizations exist for men, the question becomes, how can we reshape our way of life so that it will be more generative of human good?

What is human good? It must be something more than sheer existence, for if sheer existence is the primary characteristic, then we might as well be oysters.

I submit that human good includes the following two *minimum* components. The first is freedom from physical suffering, hunger, malnutrition, and bodily harm due to natural disaster and illness.[15] The second is freedom from boredom, purposelessness, fear of fellow men, and crippling anxiety about one's place in society.

The Chinese way of life has failed so badly with reference to the first component that traditional China was justifiably termed a land of famine. The American way of life, through its superb economic, engineering, and bio-medical achievements, is among the leaders of mankind in battling for physical comfort and fitness. But the American way of life has failed badly with reference to the second component of human good, freedom from boredom and fear. Despite spectacular success in the field of entertainment and in extending the frontiers of knowledge, still boredom, purposelessness, fear of fellow men, and anxiety are common. As a defense against these harassments, new pleasures, new goals, new enemies, and new weapons must be sought. The human environment has become so unpredictable that America may justifiably be called a land of mistrust.[16]

Since it is imperative that we live in association with other human beings, we must relate to each other not merely in terms of how *useful* we are to others, but more importantly how much *feeling* we have for them. Usefulness is a matter of skills. It can be made possible or improved by legislation, so that, for example, non-Whites can enter employment formerly reserved for Whites. But feeling is not so easily trained, for it goes to the center of our very being. It certainly cannot be made possible or improved by legislation; laws and enforcement agencies are powerless to make harmonious couples out of unloving spouses. It also cannot be improved by increasing productivity or developing resources. These remedies are means for externalizing relationships so that men will be able to disguise further their feelings for each other. We will not arrive at a new human equation in America's future unless something more fundamental is first recognized and squarely faced.

My elementary theory is that our relationship with our fellow humans, rather than our control over things, is the key to peace between human groups and happiness for the individual. Therefore, when we speak of improving the quality of life of the individual, we should be thinking of *improving the quality of interpersonal relations for the individual instead.*

If the control of material wealth remains the individual's principal investment in emotional security, Whites will be unable to surrender any substantial part of that wealth for the betterment of Blacks and the poor, and as Blacks and the poor become more affluent they will be just as reluctant to surrender any substantial part of their wealth for the benefit of other Blacks and other poor.

But somehow many *young* Americans have intuitively sensed this. If we care to understand, we can see many of their efforts as more than the negative and destructive acts of violence on campuses and in the streets. Little commune-like groups in which the members keep no private property are springing up in parts of the country. Sensitivity experiments in which participants are encouraged to touch each other under certain guises are a rage in many schools, churches, and community groups. The Living Theatre in which nearly nude or nude actors and members of the audience merge in hugging each other has been playing to full houses. The late pop-rock-soul blues singer, Janis Joplin, preached a gospel of supremacy of feeling over intellect. "Being an intellectual," said Janis, "creates a lot of questions and no answers. You can fill your life up with ideas and still go home lonely. That's what music is to me." The weekly which printed the above also reported that she made "more converts per capita than Billy Graham." [17]

These happenings, together with the widespread phenomena of anti-war sentiments and of youths discarding the comforts and status symbols of their well-to-do homes to lead socially amorphous but physically and psychologically intimate lives among strangers all point in one direction: the need of the young to relate to each other and to the rest of the world, not by wealth and superiority but by opening up their hearts; not by what one can do for the other, but by what one is to the other. This is what young Americans really mean when they say they want to be "true" and "undisguised."

However, such youthful movements, though going deeper than the notion that better and faster communications are the key to improvement of the human equation in our future, still stop at the level of symptomatic palliatives. Previously we noted that attempts at better and faster communications without the prior condition for them is self-defeating. We must now observe that the youthful activities of today will be no more than emotional massages unless we restructure our relationship with each other for greater depth and permanency.

The key to discover and implement mechanisms for developing greater depth and permanency in human relationships must be sought in the cradle of human development: the family. We need to see the family as the social germ cell, to know what psychological heredity is transmitted from generation to generation and how this is done, exactly as we study the biological germ cell and its genetic code in order to understand the processes of physical heredity.[18] We need a reassessment of our kinship system, how we as adults should behave toward our parents, how we should conduct ourselves as spouses, and what we should teach our children. Toward this end we need to divert a fraction of the colossal arms expenditure for basic researches. But these researches must not, as is so often the fashion of the day, consider the requirements of industrialization and the modern political state as absolute ends so that human beings have to be trained toward meeting them. Instead we should address ourselves to the problem of how human beings can develop and sustain feelings for each other as human beings instead of as tools. Or we must attempt to refashion industrialization and a modern political state so that their requirements will not interfere with the genesis and maintenance in human beings of feelings for each other as human beings.

The term *modernity* has been naively defined by our present-day social scientists in terms of machines and organizational efficiency for economic and political purposes. Even when they speak of the quality of human life, they still measure modernity by such things as mobility or consumption patterns. We must realize that this is no more than semimodernity at best. Freedom from want does not lead to freedom from interpersonal anxiety and hostility. But unless man achieves freedom from interpersonal apprehensions, much of what he has accomplished or will accomplish in the sphere of material well-being will be in vain, for he will only go through cycles of destruction, reconstruction—and bigger destruction and more colossal reconstruction.

In human affairs no less than in the physical world, everything has a price. The price may be money, energy, heartache, misery, revolution, war, or outright death; it may be paid by this generation or future generations, but it cannot be evaded forever. Men and women who show no respect and consideration for their own parents cannot expect their own children to treat them with respect and consideration. Nations which have ruthlessly oppressed or enforced their alleged superiority over other nations can hardly expect mercy or love from their former supposed inferiors once the shoe is on the other foot. The United States, as the most illustrious and the richest descendant of Europe, is paying and will pay a price, not in money alone, for generations of international misdeeds perpetrated by its ancestors. The modern day racial violence in our midst is but a partial payment for the 300 years of slavery suffered by the Blacks. And if the Blacks get carried away by their present hatred of the Whites and engage in enormous excesses, their children will in turn pay for such intemperance.

Before these suggested new researches are greatly under way and bear fruit, perhaps we can appeal to the rugged individual's self-interest. He should recognize that it is in his own interest—the well-being of his children and the future of his children's children—to find a new human equation for peace within the United States and in the world as a whole. The aim of this new human equation must be for man to liberate himself from the magical mode of thinking in human affairs. Once man used prayer or incantations for rain while now he builds huge dams; engaged priests and witch doctors to cure illnesses while now he makes use of x-ray and penicillin. Thanks to Western contributions to the natural sciences, the world has gradually emerged from this pre-modern notion of the magical nature of the physical universe.

But man continues to react magically to human behavior and human relations.[19] He considers it utter foolishness to build skyscrapers on sand but he still insists on building empires or alliances by forcing unwilling peoples to do his bidding. He would not now think of cheating the rockets he constructs by slipping in inferior chrome, but he still tries to pull the wool over the eyes of other humans by denying them their due and by giving out half-truths through misleading advertisements or propaganda efforts on an international scale.[20]

Above all, he is still addicted to the magic of words in human affairs.[21] Lovers under the moonlight can whisper magical words to each other. But these words will retain their magic only if there is substance in their relationship as lovers. Should we eradicate this magical mode of thinking concerning human relations? Should we stop believing we can change a saucepan into a spade because we call it a spade, a dictatorship into democracy because we call it a democracy, or a lot of irreligious frivolities into religion because we call it worship of God?

Even the rugged individual must realize that no one has a permanent tenure in life and that neither oppression nor superiority is permanent. The only permanence in life is the continuity from generation to generation. That continuity and, through it, accumulated knowledge and wisdom elevated man from the ranks of mere animals and digging sticks and gave him such things as language, literature, and rules governing human transactions. In this process each generation is at the mercy of the preceding one. We can poison the human network so that those who come after us will be burdened with a heritage of hatred and excesses because we built our happiness on other people's miseries. Or we can honestly work for a pleasant journey through this world, free from physical and psychological suffering, for ourselves and our descendants yet to come, because we have understood the truth that the pleasantness of our journey will be dependent upon how agreeable we have made it for others.

Notes

1. This article is based on two lectures I delivered: "Rugged Individualism Reconsidered," delivered at the University of Colorado and published in *The Colorado Quarterly* (Autumn 1960), pp. 143–162; and "The Human Equation in Our Future," delivered at the University of Hawaii as the third in a series of events leading up to the Governer's Conference on the Year 2000, partially published in the *Honolulu Advertiser* (March 18, 1970), under the title "Rugged Individualism Causing Crisis."

2. *Chicago Sun-Times,* April 25, 1959.

3. *Chicago Sun-Times,* August 12, 1959.

4. Edwin H. Sutherland, *White Collar Crime* (New York: Dryden Press, 1949).

5. The need for more successes to top already great successes is as American as apple pie. One can find evidence for this wherever he turns. Once, during a dinner party, my wife posed this question to a very wealthy man from Texas: "Why should you, a multimillionaire at age 63, be so concerned with making more millions?" The man's reply was candid: "I suppose it's a matter of keeping scores for myself. Besides, I love to beat [names of fellow multimillionaires in his area]."

6. David Riesman, *The Lonely Crowd* (New Haven: Yale University Press, 1952).

7. These observations were originally made in my book *Americans and Chinese: Two*

Ways of Life (New York: Abelard-Schuman, 1953), pp. 116–117. The same point was reaffirmed by Seymour Lipsett ten years later in *The First New Nation* (New York: Basic Books, 1963).

8. "The Values of American Students," in *Long Range Planning for Education* (Washington, D.C.: American Council on Education, 1958), pp. 119–120.

9. (New York: Harper Brothers, 1948).

10. It is interesting that Lionel Tiger, although arguing that bonding among males is biologically based, says that "aggression against the outside world" is its most important accompaniment. See Lionel Tiger, *Men in Groups* (New York: Random House, 1969). What the author sees is the Western but especially American behavior pattern, and he has naively taken that behavior pattern as universal.

11. *Honolulu Advertiser,* March 1, 1970. Such statements gave William L. Shirer, author of *The Rise and Fall of the Third Reich* (New York: Simon and Schuster, 1960), his fear for the "rise of Fascism in U.S." (*Honolulu Advertiser,* March 14, 1970).

12. (New York: Simon and Schuster, 1956).

13. *Popular Religion: Inspirational Books in America* (Chicago: University of Chicago Press, 1958).

14. George Homans, *The Human Group* (New York: Harcourt, Brace and Co., 1954). Homans saw this decline of small-town life as due to the desire of able men to leave it as industrialization created opportunities in the outside world. I think Homan's interpretation is culture-bound, for in other societies without rugged individualism such men may leave to make their fame and fortune elsewhere but tend to retire in the communities of their origin. See Francis L. K. Hsu, *Clan, Caste, and Club* (Princeton, N.J.: Van Nostrand, 1963), pp. 144–147.

15. Sex deprivation is, of course, also a form of physical suffering. But I do not know of any society, or a section of it, which suffers from sex deprivation other than on a voluntary basis.

16. By describing America as a land of mistrust we do not, of course, mean that all Americans are suspicious of each other, exactly as we do not imply that all Chinese were hungry because China was a land of famine.

17. *Newsweek,* January 24, 1969, p. 84.

18. A beginning in this direction has been made. See Francis L. K. Hsu, "The Effect of Dominant Kinship Relationships on Kin and Non-Kin Behavior: A Hypothesis", *American Anthropologist* 67:638–61 (1965) and Francis L. K. Hsu, ed., *Kinship and Culture,* Chicago: Aldine, 1971.

19. The popularity of UFO believers in the United States is indicative of the reality and extreme to which this mode of thinking will go. But, characteristically, the UFO devotees believe that "living" creatures inhabiting other planets—not ghosts and spirits—are manning the "crafts" from outer space.

20. It may sound fantastic, but the game theory fad which enjoys great popularity among some social scientists of today is, in my view, little more than academic wrapping for the age old magical mode of thought applied to human affairs in the same way phrenology was for palm readers and alchemy for practitioners of black arts.

21. In a way, this is the underlying assumption of those who see better communications or more researches in communication as the means for mitigating or solving problems of our time. But no amount of clarification of meaning between parents and children, Blacks and Whites, and different nations can respectively reduce the generation gap, the racial tension, and the international struggles if the two sides in each conflict harbor irreconcilable goals.

Recommended Reading

Coleman, Elizabeth, *Chinatown, U.S.A.* (New York: John Day Co., 1946). A good pictorial introduction to Chinatown today. The thirty-page text provides a brief historical background and sketch of present conditions.

Dillon, Richard H., *The Hatchet Men: The Story of the Tong Wars in San Francisco's Chinatown* (New York: Coward-McCann, 1962). A detailed history of an infamous period of San Francisco's Chinatown.

Hoy, William, *The Chinese Six Companies* (San Francisco: Chinese Consolidated Benevolent Association, 1942). A well written and accurate account of the beginning, function, and change of the most important of Chinese associations in California.

Hsu, Francis L. K., *Americans and Chinese: Purpose and Fulfillment in Great Civilizations* (New York: Natural History Press, 1970). The only book to systematically compare American and Chinese ways of life from the point of view of modern psychological anthropology. It deals with diverse subjects from art, literature, romance and hero worship, sex crime, and drug addiction to religion, economics, politics, Communism, and the generation gap. A central hypothesis brings order into seemingly chaotic facts.

Kung, Shien-woo, *Chinese in American Life: Some Aspects of Their History, Status, Problems, and Contributions* (Seattle: University of Washington Press, 1962). A storehouse of facts about the most active Chinese in the United States and their work.

La Fargue, Thomas E., *China's First Hundred* (Pullman: State College of Washington Press, 1962). A well documented account of the history of about 100 Chinese students who were the first to study in the West (U.S.A.)—except for three men who preceded them. It describes their life and work in the United States between 1871 and 1881, and the roles they played in Chinese society in the three-quarters century after their return in 1881.

Lee, Calvin, *Chinatown, U.S.A.* (Garden City, N.Y.: Doubleday & Co., 1965). A considerable description of Chinatowns in various parts of the United States, with an outline of Chinese customs, the organization of these Chinese communities, and an analysis of problems facing the Chinese in America.

Lee, Rose Hum, *The Chinese in the United States of America* (Hongkong: Hongkong University Press, 1960). This is the most comprehensive survey of the Chinese in America to date. It not only offers a wealth of data but also provides the reader with competent analyses in terms of the conceptual and methodological tools of American sociology.

Leong, Gor Yun, *Chinatown Inside Out* (New York: Barrows Mussey, 1936). A very readable insider's account of the Chinatown of New York City. It does not deal with other groups of Chinese.

Lind, Andrew W., *Hawaii's People* (Honolulu: The University of Hawaii Press, 1967). Data and analyses answering the basic questions: who are they; where do they live; how do they live; what are they becoming? Lind's conclusion is that they are all becoming one people—the Hawaiians.

Miller, Stuart Creighton, *The Unwelcome Immigrant: The American Image of the Chinese, 1785–1882* (Berkeley: University of California Press, 1969). A sound historical work detailing the pendulum-like swing of American reactions to China and Chinese immigration to the United States. The author shows how these reactions, often going abruptly from one extreme to the other, had little to do with Chinese reality. Instead, they were rooted in American fantasies, prejudices, economics, and other anxieties which are still relevant to American attitudes toward China today.

Riggs, Fred W., *Pressures on Congress: A Study of the Repeal of Chinese Exclusion* (New York: King's Crown Press, Columbia University, 1950). A study of the repeal of the Chinese exclusion law in 1943, plus an investigation of the role of the pressure groups and citizens' committees in the making of our laws.

Sparks, Theresa A., *China Gold* (Fresno, Calif.: Academy Library Guild, 1954). This is the saga of a Chinese miner in northern California during the Gold Rush days. It begins with his humble origins in Kwangtung Province, his toil as a miner amid white prejudice, marriage to a picture bride, raising a successful family, ending with the posthumous award of the Silver Star and the Purple Heart to one of his sons, 1st Lt. Albert P. Fong, killed in the Pacific May 25, 1943.

Sung, Betty Lee, *Mountains of Gold: The Story of the Chinese in America* (New York: Macmillan, 1967). A history of the Chinese in the United States from the Gold Rush to the present, including the problems of assimilation faced by Chinese–Americans from the first restrictions placed on immigration and naturalization to problems existing in today's society. It gives a good account of Chinese–American contributions in physics, biochemistry, finances, literature, cinematography, art, and architecture.

Wing, Yung, *My Life in China and America* (New York: Henry Holt and Co., 1909). An autobiography of the first Chinese student to study in the United States. It gives some insights into his problems upon returning to China. He married a white girl and later became an American citizen.

Wong, Jade Snow, *Fifth Chinese Daughter* (New York: Harper, 1950). The autobiography of a Chinese–American girl with a very interesting description of how she grew up, went to public school, learned English, and met other Americans. Like many other

Chinese–American children, she also attended Chinese school for three hours at the end of each day, so Chinese influences remained strong. However, the two ways of life brought her much stress by the time she reached high school, although she never developed permanent resentment or loss of love for her honest, kindly parents.

INDEX

Abbott, Dr. Kenneth A., 38*n*, 108*n*
Adolescence, 83–91
  delinquency, 83
  and discontinuity, 84–85
  parental control, 84–85
  peers, 85–86
Afro–Americans, 131 (*see also* Blacks)
Ai, C. K., 62
Alice in Wonderland, 1
Americanization, 111–119, 129–133
  meaning of, 112–124
  participation in, 116–119
American Dream, 123–133
Ancestor worship, 22, 23, 31, 46, 47,
  60, 63
Arranged marriage, 21, 31

Baez, Joan, 120*n*
Beatles, 17
Blacks, 1, 105–106, 123–127, 143, 148,
  149, 151*n*
Bornbush, Sanford M., 145
Brownson, Orestes, 118

Capone, Al, 140
Cause-promoting, 46
Chang, 25
Chang, the Honorable P. H., 19
Char, Dr. Donald, 9, 107*n*
Ch'en, Ta, 13
Chen-tung, Chang, 34–35
Ch'ien, Ssu-ma, 15
Chin, Pa, 16
Ching, Hung Wai, 120*n*
Chih-mo, Hsu, 16
Chinese:
  advancement, 116
  in America, 101–104
  in business, 115
  cause-promoting, 46
  children, 84–85
  Chinatown-centered, 2–3, 4, 6, 30, 31
  diversity among, 3
  in Hawaii, 2, 4–6, 48–50, 60–62
  in the media, 1

Chinese (continued)
  and friendship, 78
  inclusiveness, 62–72
  and independence, 87
  kinship, 79
  Nobel Prize winners, 6
  nonexclusiveness, 85
  scholars and professionals, 6–7
  stereotypes of, 1–2
  and Union Pacific Railroad, 104
China, 99–101, 113–124, 126, 130
  in Korea, 100
  and Chinese–Indian border dispute,
    97–98
  and Tibet, 96–97
Chinese associations, 45–49, 86 (*see*
    also Family name associations)
Chinese cemeteries, 60–62
Chinese college students, 2, 3, 9–10,
  10*n*, 35
Chinese family, 19–27, 29–38
  in America, 30–32
  dyads, 20
  generation gap, 32–37, 116, 128,
    138, 142, 151*n*
  Large Family ideal, 19–22, 23, 30
  names, 24
  obedience in, 21
  wider kinship, 23–25
Chinese funerals, 55–57
Chinese gods, 54
Chinese language, 2, 11–18
  alphabet, 14
  dialects, 11–14
  kuo yü, 13, 16
  Peking, 12
  Mandarin, 12–13
  written, 14–15, 18*n*
Chinese Six Companies, 51
Chinese tribute system, 99
Ching, Fong (Little Pete), 55–57, 60,
  65*n*
Christianity, 54–55, 65*n*, 142
  Jehovah's Witnesses, 36
Chow, Fong, 117–118

Committee on National Goals, 137
Communism, 142, 143
Conformity, 141
Confucius, 21, 27n, 50n, 54
Corruption, 140–145
Creativity, 87, 114–116, 139, 146
Crime, 19
Crisis psychology, 13
Cultural superiority, 129–130

Dever, Father, 61
Discontinuity, 83–85
Discrimination, 129–130
Dix, Dorothea, 142
Double identity, 121–123, 129–131
"Dry father," 25
Dylan, Bob, 120n

Eliot, George, 26
Emerson, Ralph Waldo, 79n
Emigration, 34, 42, 43, 50n
Er, Lee, 47
Erikson, Erik, 82
Evers, Charles, 118
Expansionism, 55, 96–101, 124
  and domino theory, 101

Family and kinship, 19–27, 69, 114
Family name associations, 32, 43–47
Farming, 39–40
Freedom, 26–27, 147, 149
Friendship, 67–79
  among Americans, 72–73, 75, 78–79
  and business, 76–77
  among Germans, 75
  and sexuality, 72–76
Fulbright, Senator J. W., 120n

Generation gap, 32–37, 116, 128, 138,
  142, 151n
Germans, 75, 96, 143
Gregory, Dick, 120n
Groppi, Father, 120n

Hall, Edward T., 143
Hatfield, Mark, 120n
Heilbroner, Robert L., 109n
Ho, Chinn, 3
Hoover, J. Edgar, 103, 104, 124

Hooverism, 104
Homans, George, 146, 151n
Hospitality, 67–79
  among Eskimos, 68–69
  among Russians, 68
  among white Americans, 67, 78–79
Howe, James Wong, 6
Hsien chu (hsien yu), 60–61
Hsueh-shen, Ch'ien, 6, 10, 100
Hsun, Lu, 16

Independence, 34, 59 (see also Rugged
  individualism)
Indians, 106, 111–112
Inouye, Senator Daniel K., 12n
Intermarriage, 5–6, 31, 120n
Irish–Americans, 131
Islam, 143
Israel, Mrs. John, 10n, 92n, 107n, 108n
Italian–Americans, 131

Jackson, Andrew, 118
Japanese, 13, 16, 71, 96, 102, 127
Jefferson, Thomas, 118
Jen ch'ing wei, 67, 77, 79
Jesus, 41–42
Jews, 1, 43, 53, 70, 102, 105, 106,
  123–125, 129–130, 143
Juvenile delinquency, 114
Joplin, Janis, 148
Jow, Harold, 61

Kai, General Ts'ai T'ing, 9
Kellogg, Mary Louise, 31
Kennedy, John F., 127
King, Martin Luther, 118
Kingman, Dong, 6
Kinship, 43–46, 59, 85–86
Ku Klux Klan, 48
Kuan, 25
Kung Ch'ang tu Association, 125
Kuo yü, 13, 16
Kuomintang, 3, 63
Kwock, Reverend Charles, 61

Lee, Calvin, 129
Lee, Chin Y., 6
Lee, Robert, 6
Lee, Dr. Rose Hum, 9

Legislative Committee of the Church-
men's Commission for Decent
Publications, 140
Lewin, Kurt, 74, 123–124, 143
Liang, T'an-kung, 47
Lincoln, Abraham, 118
Little Pete (see Ching, Fong)
Liu, 25
Liu, Clarence, 61
Liu, Dr. Ta-ching, 3
Local ties, 39–50
Locality associations, 45, 125
Lum, Chung Park, 88–90
Lung, Dean, 117–118, 125
Lyman, Stanford M., 103

MacArthur, General Douglas, 100
Mafia, 48, 51n
Malik, Charles, 137
Michener, James A., 117
Milton, John, 75, 76
Mo-jo, Kuo, 16, 31

Needham, Joseph, 14
Negroes (see Blacks)
Noah and the ark, 40–42, 54, 58
Norris, Frank, 56

Organization of Chinese, 46–50

Pacific Club, 48–49
Pai hua, 16–17
Park, Dr. Robert E., 91n
Parry, Joseph, 79n
Paulinus, 75
Pei, I. M., 6
Persecution, 103
Poitier, Sydney, 1
Polish–Americans, 131
Pollution, 138
Pornography, 139–140
Prejudice, 95–108, 127, 141–142
Psychic baggage, 69–70

Racial tension, 138
Racism (see Prejudice)
Red Guards, 85, 89n–90n
Religion, 53–64, 87, 91n–92n
    cemeteries, 63
    among Chinese in America, 60–62
    Christianity, 61–62

Religion (continued)
    mixing of, among Chinese, 62–64
    multiplicity of gods, 53–57
    persecution, 58–60
Riesman, David, 141
Robinson, Joan, 107n
Rousseau, Jean Jacques, 144
Rugged individualism, 39–40, 137–150
Russian–Americans, 131

Salinger, J. D., 76
Schneider, Louis, 145
Self-reliance (see Rugged individual-
    ism)
Sex ratio, 5, 10n
Sexual morality, 139–140
Sexuality, 72–76, 151n
Shih, Dr. Hsu, 16
Shirer, William L., 151n
Shun, Emperor, 41, 44
Social baggage, 69–70
Spender, Stephen, 80n
Spock, Dr. Benjamin, 120n
Ssu Ta Tu Association, 125
Steinbeck, John, 76
Stowe, Harriet Beecher, 118
Suchman, Edward S., 141
Suspicion, 142–143, 151n
Swedish–Americans, 131

T'an-Kung, Liang, 47
Taylor, Elizabeth, 57
Tennyson, Alfred Lord, 75
Thoreau, Henry David, 83, 118
Tiger, Lionel, 151n
T'ing-Kai, Ts'ai, 115
Tocqueville, Alexis de, 116
Todd, Michael, 57
Tongs, 46, 48, 51n, 127
Ts'ai, Gerald, 6
Tsin, Char Nyuk, 117
Turner, Frederick J., 39

Unfilialness, 33–34
Union of South Africa, 105–106

Van Dyke, Henry, 75
Vietnam War, 21, 95–96, 101, 118
Violence, 138

Walker, Ted, 80
White supremacy, 129

Whyte, William H., 144
Wing, Yung, 31
Women, 20–21, 23, 26, 130
Wong, Worley K., 6
Wriston, Dr. Henry, 137

Yale University, 129
Yao, Emperor, 41
Yat-sen, Dr. Sun, 42
Yu, 58
Yu, Emperor, 41

58147